D0417301

rose elliot's
mediterranean
feasts

rose elliot's
mediterranean
feasts

Little Books by Big Names™

First published in the United Kingdom in 2004 by Little Books Ltd,
48 Catherine Place, London SW1E 6HL

10 9 8 7 6 5 4 3 2 1

A CIP catalogue record for this book is available from the British Library.
Some of the recipes in this book previously appeared in
Forget the Lentils, Little Books 2003.

ISBN: 1 904435 33 5

The author and publisher will be grateful for any information that will
assist them in keeping future editions up-to-date. Although all reasonable care
has been taken in the preparation of this book, neither the publisher, editors nor
the author can accept any liability for any consequences arising from the use
thereof, or the information contained therein.

Many thanks to: Jamie Ambrose for editorial production and management,
Claudia Dowell for proofreading, Two Associates for jacket design,
Mousemat Design for text design, Craig Campbell of QSP Print
for printing consultancy. Printed and bound in Scotland by Scotprint.

contents

*A good cook is like a sorceress who
dispenses happiness.*

Elsa Schiapirelli

introduction

Mediterranean Feasts is a book that puts summer back into eating. Today it is possible to enjoy fresh flavours, easy cooking and maximum sunshine all year round: to eat the foods that have evolved naturally in the sunny countries of the Med, and so are perfect for hot, lazy days and long, warm evenings. This book has been built around the foods that are ideal at such times. It features dishes made from ingredients that are in season and abundant: food that is as enjoyable *al fresco* as it is for indoor dining, for nibbling with drinks or savouring around a candlelit table.

Those of us who have been lucky enough to spend time in Mediterranean countries have many happy memories that are evoked by these foods and the dishes made from them. I only have to look at, say, a flaky filo and spinach pie or a dish of crisply fried aubergine, and I'm in Greece, feeling tanned and relaxed, sipping ouzo under a star-studded sky, the air heavy with the scent of thyme and the sound of cicadas. Similarly, tasting a sun-ripened tomato salad or inhaling the whiff of garlic always transports me to the south of France.

In this book you will find a collection of dishes which I think are most evocative of the Mediterranean. I have divided them into fairly loose sections according to when you might be most likely to use them; however, there is a certain amount of overlap because the recipes are so versatile. Those listed in the 'Tapas' chapter are mainly nibbles and dips, yet they can double as a main meal, especially if you serve a selection. This is the kind of relaxed, easy food that's exactly right for hot weather.

The same can be said of the 'Summer Soups and Salads' chapter – the title says it all. Here you'll find some recipes that are great for lunches, starters and accompaniments, as well as light meals. 'Sunny

Snacks and Suppers' focuses on the kind of main courses that appeal when the temperature rises, while 'Al Fresco' takes the action outside, with food for picnics, barbecues and open-air parties. And of course, there is a chapter on puddings. They speak for themselves, featuring such quick and easy delights as sun-ripened summer fruits, easy ice cream and more exotic sorbets. You'll also find some refreshing seasonal drinks among the recipes, both with and without alcohol.

All of the recipes in this book are perfect for making in summer, since the ingredients on which they're based are in season, and people's appetites naturally crave hot-weather food. However, I also love to make them in winter. In fact, I think I almost appreciate them more then. When the sky is leaden, the wind biting and the pavements grey, I find that the clove-like fragrance of basil lifts the spirits as I take it out of my shopping bag and start crushing garlic, deseeding juicy red peppers, slicing aubergines. And as the oven heats up and those Mediterranean aromas fill the kitchen, who could fail to feel cheered, and reminded of the promise of the sun's return?

store-cupboard essentials

It pays to have a quick check in your kitchen store cupboard before you go shopping. Once you've got in the basic packets and jars, you can top them up as stocks get low; then pick up some fresh produce, and you're ready to cook. The basics are listed below.

dry goods
chocolate
Keep a good dark one with seventy percent cocoa solids; also white chocolate for more indulgent recipes.

couscous and bulgur wheat
Both of these keep well and only need soaking and heating for quick, easy accompaniments to vegetable dishes and as a basis for salads such as tabbouleh.

digestive biscuits
To make a base for cheesecakes and tortes.

dried beans and lentils
Wonderful for cheap, filling, traditional country dishes.

flour
Buy small bags of both plain and self-raising.

nuts
Almonds, pine nuts and walnuts. For freshness, store in the freezer; they don't need thawing before use.

pasta
Buy your favourites such as spaghetti, rigatoni, penne, farfalle, fettucine, tagliatelle, linguine and pappardelle.

polenta
Buy the powder, not the ready-made dough, and follow the packet directions.

porcini, dried
These are very useful for intensifying flavours in many mushroom dishes.

rice
Keep basmati on hand (it cooks in just ten minutes) as well as a good risotto rice – carnaroli or arborio.

sugar
Caster has a mellower flavour. Light-brown sugar is sometimes useful for puddings.

sun-dried or sun-blush tomatoes
Essential in many modern Mediterranean dishes. These are usually found in a packet near the porcini.

condiments and spices

bay leaves
A herb that improves with drying, so they're easy to keep on hand.

bouillon powder
Try Marigold Vegetable Bouillon, now available in most supermarkets as well as health-food shops. When I say 'stock', this is what I mean, dissolved in water.

cardamom
One of the lesser-used spices, but it's a lovely one to have on hand and use more often if you like.

chillies, chilli flakes
A jar of dried red chillies or chilli flakes is handy.

cinnamon
The powdered type.

cumin or cumin seeds
I love the flavour, so it's in quite a few recipes.

curry powder
Useful for a quick, spicy flavouring.

nutmeg
Keep as ready-ground, but freshly grated nutmegs yield a better flavour.

pepper
Buy spare black peppercorns for your grinder.

saffron
I usually buy a jar from the supermarket spice rack. It's fine – though expensive.

salt
I like Maldon sea salt, which you can scrunch over food with your fingers.

turmeric
Lovely in curries and so good for you, too! Studies have shown that turmeric benefits everything from blood sugar to liver function.

jars and bottles

artichoke hearts in oil
Great for adding to cooked pasta or salads.

black olives
Loose at supermarket delis or Middle Eastern shops.

capers
These come either salted or packed in vinegar. Rinse the salted ones thoroughly before use.

mayonnaise
Buy the best quality you can afford.

olive oil
Use extra-virgin for salad dressings; a lighter type for shallow-frying (or use rape-seed oil: see page 17).

red peppers
A very useful item to have in the store-cupboard. A jar of these, well-drained, can replace grilled peppers in some recipes such as the cannellini bean and pepper dip on page 24.

sherry, madeira and vermouth
Pretty interchangeable here – and you don't have to open a bottle of wine every time you make a risotto.

stem ginger
The kind in syrup in a pretty jar, for some puddings.

tabasco sauce
This is one of those magic ingredients that really perks things up.

truffle oil
In a small bottle from good supermarkets. Gives an earthy, sexy flavour to bland foods.

vegetable oil
Rape-seed is best for deep-frying, as it's the most stable of all oils at high temperatures.

vinegar
Red-wine vinegar is a basic staple. I like the lightness of rice vinegar, while cider vinegar tastes good and is traditionally thought to have health-giving properties.

chilled or dairy
butter
Buy organic, if possible.

cream and yogurt
Again, it's worth getting organic if you can.

chilled pastry
From any supermarket. Ready-rolled makes life easier.

cheese
Buy according to the recipe and keep well-wrapped in the fridge. Have some fresh Parmesan to hand. Vegetarian cheeses are marked.

eggs
Buy free-range, organic. Size isn't important as far as these recipes are concerned.

bread
If your freezer is big enough. Choose from a packet of pitta bread, a baguette or ficelle, or some nice Italian bread, as well as a basic loaf.

cans
beans and chickpeas
Cannellini beans and chickpeas are always useful items to have on hand, as are flageolet beans, if you can find them. One 400–420g (14–15oz) can is the equivalent of 100g (3½oz) dried beans.

condensed milk
This is a terrific item to have on hand for emergencies – such as the time you want to make that one very indulgent ice-cream recipe...

tomatoes
Organic tomatoes have no added citric acid. It's useful to have whole and chopped ones available.

fresh produce

Most fresh produce you'd buy when it was needed, according to what you are planning to cook, but a few basics are always useful.

chillies
I love the long, slim red ones that aren't too hot. They often come in packs, so put any leftovers in the freezer.

garlic
An everyday essential. Buy juicy, plump bulbs.

ginger
Keep a big chunk of this in the fridge.

herbs
Buy as required.

lemons
A splash of fresh lemon juice will perk up any dish.

onions
Along with garlic, onions are the flavouring ingredient I use for most dishes.

essential equipment

Many traditional cooks in the Mediterranean rely on very simple equipment. A really good knife is top of the list and always well worth tracking down. My favourite everyday, all-purpose knife is a Sabatier with an 18cm (seven-inch) blade. It's not stainless, so it's a curse to clean, but it does mean I can keep it sharp more easily.

To go with the knife, you need a good chopping board: big and thick. I have to have wood. And you'd be surprised how much you use a really good potato peeler. I prefer a swivel-bladed one with a handle that you can hold like a knife, though some people prefer chunkier ones.

You also need an efficient grater. I'm devoted to my 'box' grater, which has a sharp slicing edge and nice open holes, one large set for grating things like cheese and carrots, and some small ones for lemon rind or even garlic. I also like a fine, ultra-sharp Microplane grater, which I find magical for grating garlic instead of crushing it; it's also excellent for ginger.

When it comes to food processors, of course you can survive without one, but if you like cooking, it saves a lot of time. If you're just buying one, opt for a decent make that's simple to use but doesn't try to do too much. Whisking, for instance, is best done with an electric hand whisk (surprisingly cheap). I must have become quite lazy, because I really love my electric lemon-squeezer, which sits on my work surface and produces juice at the touch of a cut lemon half.

Good pans are another essential, and here, you really get what you pay for. I prefer stainless steel. Wooden spoons, a good sieve, a colander, measuring spoons and a jug, and some scales should round out your basic equipment essentials.

Finally – and we're talking big stuff here – if you're getting a new fridge, be sure that it's a large one. In an ideal world, make it two. If I had to choose between them, I'd rather have a large fridge and a small freezer. A big fridge really does save time, because it means you can buy all your fresh vegetables, herbs, cheese and so on for the week in one go and know they'll be as bright and perky on Friday evening as they were on Saturday when you put them in.

The whole Mediterranean – the sculpture, the palm, the gold beads, the bearded heroes, the wine, the ideas, the ships, the moonlight, the winged gorgons, the bronze men, the philosophers... all of it seems to rise in the sour, pungent taste of those black olives. A taste older than meat, older than wine. A taste as old as cold water.

Lawrence Durrell,
Prospero's Cell

1

tapas

Have you ever idled away a long summer's evening, sitting by the harbour-side, listening to the lapping of the water, watching as the lights come on and the stars begin to stud the sky? All the time drinking the local wine or some icy, aniseedy liquid with a plate of coloured tapas before you and not a care in the world? Me, too. And do you sometimes, perhaps on a grey, British summer's day, or even in the middle of winter, want to re-create that sunny, carefree mood? Well, with the recipes in this section, it can be done. Just put together two or three, open a bottle and relax. It's a great way to entertain.

avocado dip

Avocado dip is essentially just avocado mashed or puréed with anything you want to put with it. To make it into more of a guacamole, use only finely chopped tomatoes, chillies, coriander leaves and salt and pepper; for a smooth, simple dip, just mash or mix the avocado with lime or lemon juice, garlic and seasoning. Serve as a dip or top a salad with billowing spoonfuls of it for a luxurious creamy dressing.

serves 4

small bunch or packet of coriander, chopped

4 tomatoes, finely chopped

1 green chilli, deseeded and finely chopped

2 large avocados

salt and freshly ground black pepper

lemon or lime juice

1 This is best if you can start it about an hour before you want to eat it. Put the coriander, tomatoes and chilli into a bowl, mix and set aside.

2 Just before you want to serve the dip, halve, skin and stone the avocados, then mash them into the coriander mixture. You can do this by hand with a fork for a fairly coarse texture, or transfer everything to a food processor and pulse a few times until it's the consistency you want.

3 Finally, season with salt and freshly ground black pepper. If you're keeping the dip for any length of time, squeeze in a little lemon or lime juice to help preserve the colour; it tastes good, too.

When the Super Bowl comes, there is going to be thievery. People want guacamole.
From an article on avocado theft,
New York Times

cannellini bean & roasted pepper dip

serves 4

1 large red pepper

420g or 14–15oz can cannellini beans

1 garlic clove, crushed

2 tablespoons fresh lemon juice

salt and freshly ground black pepper

*Food is the poetry of the mouth,
in its combinations comes
the exquisite tastes of life.*

D. Lester Young

1 Set the grill on high. Halve the red pepper right down through the stalk end, then remove the stalk, seeds and core.

2 Put the pepper halves, cut-side down, on a grill pan and grill them for ten to fifteen minutes, until the skin has blistered and charred in places and the flesh is tender. Cool slightly, then cut up roughly and put into a food processor.

3 Drain the cannellini beans, saving the liquid. Add the beans to the red pepper in the food processor, along with the garlic and lemon juice. Whizz to a thick purée, then add enough of the reserved liquid to make a creamy consistency.

4 Season with salt and pepper.

goats cheese dip

serves 4

2 x 100g or 3½oz packets soft white goats cheese

1 garlic clove, crushed

2–3 tablespoons chopped fresh herbs: parsley,
   chives, dill, oregano – all or some

pinch of chilli powder or cayenne
   pepper, optional

sea salt and freshly ground black pepper

1 Put the cheese into a bowl, then stir in one or two
   tablespoons of hot water to give it the necessary
   soft, 'dipping' consistency.

2 Mix in the garlic, herbs, chilli powder or cayenne,
   along with the sea salt and freshly ground black
   pepper to taste.

3 Spoon into a small bowl to serve.

marinated olives

handful of assorted olives – purpley Kalamatas,
    big green ones, little black niçoise

3 garlic cloves, sliced

1 teaspoon ground cumin

1 teaspoon red chilli flakes

freshly ground black pepper

olive oil

1 Put the olives into a bowl. Add the garlic, cumin,
  chilli and a good grinding of black pepper.

2 Pour over enough olive oil to cover and leave to
  marinade for at least two hours.

grilled garlic flatbreads

Quick to do, these make a tempting starter to nibble while the rest of the food is cooking. Try them with one of the dips on pages 22–6.

serves 4

4 tablespoons olive oil

2 garlic cloves, peeled and finely chopped

1 tablespoon chopped flat-leaf parsley

sea salt and freshly ground black pepper

4 flat sesame or white pitta breads

1 Mix together the olive oil, garlic, parsley and a little salt and pepper – this is the topping for the breads. Make cuts 1cm (half a inch) apart on the top of each pitta bread without cutting right through into the second layer.

2 To grill the garlic breads, put the breads on the barbecue grill with the cut-side down; grill for one to two minutes. Flip the pittas over, spoon the olive oil mixture over the cut top and cook for a further one to two minutes until piping hot all through.

3 Alternatively, to cook in the oven, bake for five to ten minutes at 200°C (400°F or gas mark 6); or cook them under the grill doing the uncut side first, then turning them over, spooning the olive oil and garlic mixture on top, and grilling again.

Without garlic, I simply would not care to live.
Louis Diat

vegetarian tapenade

*Many tapenades contain anchovies; this is a
vegetarian version. You can make this more
elaborate with some chopped fresh herbs
and crushed garlic if you like.*

serves 4–6

175g or 6oz pitted black olives

1 tablespoon capers, rinsed

2 teaspoons olive oil

dash of Tabasco

salt and pepper

1 Put the stoned olives into a food processor with the
capers and olive oil and whizz to a purée.

2 Add Tabasco and salt and pepper to taste.

french tabbouleh

This is the way the French do it – or at least a French friend of mine. Very easy and full of flavour.

serves 4

225g or 8oz couscous

2 tablespoons chopped parsley

2 tablespoons chopped mint

4 spring onions, chopped

4 tomatoes, chopped

½ cucumber, diced

juice of ½ lemon

2 tablespoons olive oil

salt and freshly ground black pepper

lemon slices and olives, to garnish

Put all the ingredients into a bowl and mix together, adding salt and pepper to taste. Cover and leave in the fridge for eight to twelve hours, or overnight.

greek butterbeans

This is a recipe for gigantes, those delicious beans in tomato sauce that you can find at any taverna in Greece; I love them. This makes a lot, but leftovers freeze well.

serves 6–8

500g or 1lb 2oz butterbeans

4 large tomatoes, chopped

1 onion, sliced

3 garlic cloves, chopped

2 carrots, sliced

2 sticks of celery, chopped

6 tablespoons olive oil

salt and pepper

1 Soak the butterbeans in plenty of cold water for eight hours or overnight. Drain, and simmer them in water to cover until tender – about one hour. Drain, season with salt and pepper and put into a shallow oiled casserole.

2 Mix together the tomatoes, onion, garlic, carrots, celery and olive oil; season with salt and pepper. Spoon this mixture on top of the beans, so that they are covered.

3 Bake at 180°C (350°F or gas mark 4) for about forty minutes, or until the vegetables are tender and the beans are bathed in a tomato sauce.

4 Serve at room temperature, with plenty of bread.

Some people are fat, some people are lean.
But I want you to show me the person
who doesn't like butterbeans...

B-52s
'Butterbean'

provençal lentils

This is wonderful as a tapas, with good bread and extra olive oil.

serves 4–6

1 tablespoon olive oil

1 onion, sliced

1 garlic clove, finely chopped

pinch or two of dried, crushed red chillies

250g or 9oz Puy lentils

750ml or 26fl oz water

juice and grated rind of 1 lemon

salt and freshly ground black pepper

extra olive oil, to serve

chopped flat-leaf parsley

1 Heat the oil in a roomy saucepan. Put in the onion, cover and cook gently for about seven minutes, then add the garlic and fry for a few more seconds.

2 Add the chillies, lentils and water; bring to the boil, then leave to cook, half covered, for twenty-five to thirty minutes, or until the lentils are tender. Add more water during this time if needed.

3 Add the lemon rind and juice, and salt and pepper to taste. Serve hot or cold, with extra olive oil and the parsley sprinkled over the top.

If Leekes you like, but do their smell dis-like,
Eat Onyons, and you shall not smell the Leeke;
If you of Onyons would the scent expell,
Eat Garlicke, that shall drowne the Onyons' smell.
                                    Dr William Kitchiner
                                    The Cook's Oracle, 1831

aubergine & black olive tapenade rolls

serves 4–6

2 aubergines

2 tablespoons olive oil

for the tapenade
175g or 6oz pitted black olives

1 tablespoon capers, rinsed

2 teaspoons olive oil

thick Greek yogurt, to serve

The olive tree is surely the richest gift of Heaven.
Thomas Jefferson

1 Put the grill on high.

2 Cut the stalk ends from the aubergines, then slice the aubergines lengthwise into slices about 3mm (⅛ inch) thick. You will probably get eight to ten slices.

3 Brush the slices lightly on both sides with olive oil and place side by side on a grill pan. Grill for about five minutes, or until pale brown on top, then turn them over and grill the other side until that, too, is lightly browned and the aubergine is tender when pierced with a sharp knife. Leave to cool.

4 Meanwhile, make the tapenade. Put the stoned olives into a food processor with the capers and olive oil and whizz to a purée.

5 To make the rolls, spread the top of one of the aubergine slices quite thinly with tapenade, then roll it up firmly like a swiss roll. Place seam-side down on a plate. Continue in this way until you have done them all. Serve with a bowl of thick Greek yogurt.

roasted almonds

These golden-brown, crisp almonds are delectable.
Although you can buy them, homemade ones are
so much nicer. They're easy to do, and irresistible,
– especially when still warm.

serves 4–6

175g or 6oz almonds

1 teaspoon olive oil

1½ teaspoons sea salt

> *Almond blossom, sent to teach us*
> *That the spring days soon will reach us.*
> Edwin Arnold
> 'Almond Blossoms'

1 Put the almonds into a saucepan, cover with water and bring to the boil. Boil for two minutes, then drain into a sieve. Cool a little, then slip off the brown skins with your fingers.

2 Preheat the oven to 150°C (300°F or gas mark 2).

3 Put the almonds on a baking sheet, add the oil and rub the almonds in it with your fingers so that they all get coated. Spread them out in a single layer.

4 Bake the almonds for about twenty to twenty-five minutes, or until golden and crisp. Remove from the oven and tip onto a piece of greaseproof paper; don't leave them on the baking sheet because they will continue cooking.

5 Sprinkle with the salt and leave to cool.

chickpea &
spinach tapas

Frozen chopped spinach can be used instead of fresh spinach; all you need to do is to allow it to thaw, then drain well.

serves 4–6

250g or 9oz ready-to-cook spinach

400g or 14oz can chickpeas, drained

1 garlic clove, crushed

2–4 tablespoons fresh lemon juice

4 tablespoons olive oil

1 red pepper, deseeded and finely chopped

salt and pepper

1 Rinse the spinach, then cook in just the water clinging to it for four to five minutes, or until tender. Drain well.

2 Put the spinach into a food processor along with the chickpeas and garlic, and whizz to a purée. Add two tablespoons of the lemon juice and all of the oil, and whizz again,

3 Stir in the red pepper and salt and pepper. Taste, and add more lemon juice if needed.

4 Serve with crackers.

The disappearance of hot hors-d'oeuvre was the result of the excessive development of women's skirts.

Baron Leon Brisse

spanish omelette

Everyone loves this, and it's so versatile: equally delicious served hot, warm or cold. Cut into little pieces and served as a nibble or tapas, or slice it into generous wedges, with some salad, as a main course.

serves 8

3–4 tablespoons olive oil

1 onion, chopped

3 large baking potatoes, peeled and sliced thinly

3 eggs, beaten

salt and pepper

chopped parsley to garnish

Love and eggs are best when they are fresh.
Russian proverb

1 Heat three tablespoons of the olive oil in a frying pan. Add the onions and fry for five minutes, then add the potato and fry for a further ten minutes or so, until the potato is tender and browning at the edges. Season with salt and pepper.

2 Spread the potato and onion mixture evenly over the base of the frying pan. Season the beaten eggs, then pour into the pan on top of the potatoes, so that they are covered. Move the potatoes gently to allow the egg to flow underneath them.

3 Fry over a gentle heat until the egg has set around the edges, then loosen the omelette with a spatula, invert the frying pan over a large plate and turn the omelette out.

4 Add the rest of the oil to the pan, then slide the omelette back into the pan to cook the other side. When the omelette is set, and both sides golden brown, remove from the heat.

5 Let it cool in the pan for five to ten minutes – or completely if you wish – then sprinkle with chopped parsley, cut into small pieces and serve.

cherry tomatoes
stuffed with tapenade

serves 6–8

24 cherry tomatoes

vegetarian tapenade, page 30

chopped parsley, to garnish

1 Using a sharp, serrated knife, cut the top off each cherry tomato and also carefully slice a little from the base so that they will stand level.

2 With a pointed teaspoon or the point of the knife, scoop out the centres of the tomatoes – you don't have to use this, though you could chop some of it and add to the tapenade if you wish.

3 Season the tomatoes with salt and pepper, then stuff with tapenade and garnish with parsley.

garlic bread

serves 6

125g or 4oz soft butter

3–4 garlic cloves, crushed

1 large baguette

1 Preheat the oven to 200°C (400°F or gas mark 6).

2 Beat the butter with the garlic. Slice the baguette at 2.5cm (one-inch) intervals, without cutting right through the bottom.

3 Pull back the pieces and spread the cut sides with the garlic butter. Put onto a baking tray and bake for fifteen to twenty minutes until it's piping hot, crisp and oozing garlicky butter.

rosemary & raisin bread

350g or 12oz strong, unbleached white flour

10g or ¼oz sachet dried, easy-blend yeast

2 teaspoons salt

1 teaspoon sugar

225ml or 8fl oz warm water

a little extra flour for kneading, as necessary

olive oil

55g or 2oz raisins

1 tablespoon dried rosemary

2–3 teaspoons coarse sea salt, for topping

What hymns are sung, what praises said
For homemade miracles of bread.

Louis Untermeyer

1 Put the flour, yeast, salt and sugar into a bowl, add the warm water and mix with your hands, a wooden spoon or in a food processor until a dough forms.

2 Knead the dough by hand for five minutes on a clean surface, flouring as necessary to prevent sticking.

3 Oil the surface of the dough lightly with your hands, place it in a deep bowl, stretch some clingfilm over the top and leave in a warm place until it has doubled in size: one to two hours, depending on the temperature.

4 Punch down the dough, add the raisins and rosemary, knead for one to two minutes, put it back into the bowl as before and leave to rise again. This time it will only take about forty-five minutes.

5 Knead lightly and roll out in a circle or oval that will fit on your barbecue grill. I cook it straight on a fine-mesh grill (well-oiled) over the barbecue.

6 Cook the bread until the underside is golden brown – about ten minutes – then flip it over, sprinkle the uncooked side with sea salt, brush with olive oil, and cook in the same way.

piquant onion tarts

2 tablespoons olive oil

4 red onions, sliced

500g or 1lb 2oz ready-made puff pastry

2 tablespoons pine nuts

2 tablespoons capers

2 tablespoons chopped sun-dried tomatoes

2 tablespoons chopped pitted black olives

125g or 4oz feta cheese, diced

1 tablespoon chopped rosemary (optional)

salt and freshly ground black pepper

1 Preheat the oven to 220°C (425°F or gas mark 7).

2 Heat the oil in a large saucepan. Put in the onions, cover, and cook gently for fifteen minutes, stirring occasionally. Remove from the heat.

3 Roll out the pastry on a floured surface and cut into four 15cm (six-inch) circles; prick with a fork. Put into the fridge to chill briefly.

4 Stir the nuts, capers, tomatoes, olives, cheese and rosemary (if using) into the onions; season. Put the pastry circles on a baking sheet, then top with the onion mixture, leaving about 1cm (half an inch) clear around the edges.

5 Bake for about fifteen minutes, or until the pastry is golden and puffed up. Serve at once.

A man hath no better thing under the sun,
than to eat, and to drink, and to be merry.
Ecclesiastes 8:15

asparagus with quick hollandaise sauce

serves 6

2 bunches of asparagus

125g or 4oz butter, in chunks

2 free-range egg yolks

1 tablespoon fresh lemon juice

salt and freshly ground black pepper

Eggs are very much like small boys. If you overheat them, or overbeat them, they will turn on you, and no amount of future love will right the wrong.

Anonymous

1 Bend the asparagus stems, letting them break where they will; discard the tough ends and wash the rest. Cut into 3cm (about one-inch) lengths.

2 Cook the asparagus in a little boiling water for three to four minutes, until the stems are only just tender, and then drain.

3 In a saucepan, melt the butter over a gentle heat, without browning it. Put the egg yolks, lemon juice and some seasoning into a food processor or blender and whizz for one minute, until thick.

4 With the machine running, pour in the melted butter in a thin, steady stream, and the sauce will thicken. Allow to stand for a minute or two, then serve while still hot, with the hot asparagus.

tuscan tomato bruschette

Bruschette make excellent starters or crunchy accompaniments to grilled food and are easy to make. In Italy, panne rustica would be used, but this is difficult to obtain and I find a granary or wholewheat loaf makes a good substitute.

makes 4

4 slices of bread

olive oil, for brushing

1 garlic clove, peeled and halved

for the tomato and basil topping

450g or 1lb tomatoes, skinned and chopped

salt and freshly ground black pepper

4 sprigs of fresh basil

1 Lay slices of bread on a barbecue grill (or griddle or grill-pan if cooking indoors), turning it over to toast each side – it will only take a minute or two.

2 Immediately rub the garlic over the surface of the bread and drizzle with a little olive oil.

3 Spoon some of the tomatoes on top of each, season with salt and pepper and top with some torn basil leaves. Serve immediately.

other toppings

Sun-dried tomato and feta cheese
Good-quality sun-dried tomato purée makes a good topping. Spread it lightly over the bruschette and top with a little crumbled feta cheese.

Avocado with rocket
Halve an avocado, remove the stone and cut the avocado into quarters. Mash it roughly with a squeeze of lemon juice and sea salt and pepper to taste, or use guacamole (see page 22). Top the bruschette with the avocado and a few rocket leaves dipped lightly in vinaigrette.

flaky spinach & fennel pastries

makes 20

8 sheets filo pastry

75g or about 3oz butter or vegan
  margarine, melted

for the filling

1 onion, peeled and finely chopped

1 tablespoon olive oil

225g or 8oz cooked fresh spinach, well-drained
  and chopped, or frozen spinach, thawed and
  squeezed as dry as possible

2 tablespoons chopped parsley

1 teaspoon fennel seed

salt and freshly ground black pepper

1 To make the filling: fry the onion in the olive oil in a large saucepan until soft but not browned. Add the cooked spinach, chopped parsley and fennel seed. Mix well, then season to taste with salt and pepper.

2 Preheat the oven to 190°C (375°F or gas mark 5).

3 Unroll the sheets of filo pastry; spread them out flat in a pile with a damp cloth over them. Take one sheet, spread it out on a board and brush the top surface all over with melted butter. Lay another pastry sheet on top, brush with more butter, then make four equally spaced cuts from one short end of the sheet to the other; you should end up with five long strips.

4 Place a teaspoon of filling about 2.5cm (one inch) from the top of one strip. Fold one of the top corners over it to make a triangle. Then fold the triangle down from the base, then at an angle again. Continue in this way until you end up with a neat layered triangle. Place on a baking sheet. Continue with the rest of the filo and filling until everything is used up, then brush the triangles all over with butter.

5 Bake about fifteen minutes, or until the pastry is golden-brown and crisp, and the filling is piping hot.

fresh dates stuffed with feta & mint

These are sweet yet refreshing: lovely as part of a selection of savoury tapas but equally good served towards the end for a sweet finale.

serves 4–6

225g or 8oz fresh dates

125g or 4oz feta, diced

small bunch of mint leaves

1 Make a cut down one side of each date and remove the stone.

2 Carefully push a mint leaf and a piece of feta into each date, to replace the stone, and gently press the dates together again.

3 Serve the dates piled up on a small plate, perhaps decorated with a few remaining leaves or sprigs of mint. Or line the plate with fresh green leaves – mint or fig, if available – before putting the dates on it.

raisin bread, goats cheese & fig bites

Another sweet-and-savoury idea. The combination of a sweet, perhaps slightly malty, bread with the tangy goats cheese and ripe fig is great. The cocktail sticks are optional but they do make them easier to eat.

serves 4–6

a few slices of raisin, fruit or malt bread

125g or 4oz smooth goats cheese

1 ripe fig

cocktail sticks, optional

1 Spread the slices of bread quite thickly with the goats cheese, then cut each into quarters (or more) to make pieces about 2.5cm (one inch) square.

2 Cut the fig into slivers to fit the squares and place a piece of fig on each. Spear a cocktail stick right through the centre of each if you like, to make it easier to pick up.

It takes four men to dress a salad: a wise man for the salt, a madman for the pepper, a miser for the vinegar, and a spendthrift for the oil.

Anonymous

summer soups
& salads

These recipes are so versatile. Many of them can be
served equally well as first courses, main courses or
side dishes, depending on the occasion and what
else you're going to eat. I must say I particularly like
the summer soups: a chilled soup makes such a
refreshing start to a summer meal, while a hot one
can turn a simple salad meal into a filling feast. And
some of the soups can be served either hot or cold,
according to the weather – or your mood when the
moment comes. Equally, there are both warm and
cold salads here, and a wide variety of ingredients –
something for everyone, I hope.

white gazpacho

*It's white, it's chilled, it's delicious and it's from Spain –
but there the similarity to the red gazpacho we know
and love ends. This is a wonderful, piquant mixture of
sweet and sour: a heavenly dish on a hot day.*

serves 4

200g or 7oz whole almonds

2 slices white or wholemeal bread, crusts removed

2 garlic cloves, crushed

3 tablespoons sherry vinegar or balsamic vinegar

600ml or 20fl oz ice water

sea salt and freshly ground black pepper

250g or 9oz sweet, green seedless grapes, halved

1 Put the almonds into a small saucepan, cover with water and boil for one minute. Drain and slip the skins off the almonds.

2 Put the almonds into a food processor with the bread, garlic and vinegar. Whizz very thoroughly, until the almonds are as fine as you can get them, then add a little ice water to make a paste and whizz again. Gradually add the rest of the water until you have a gorgeously creamy mixture. Season with salt and pepper. Chill until required.

3 To serve, divide the grapes among four chilled bowls and ladle the soup on top.

Tastes are made, not born.

Mark Twain

fresh tomato soup with farfalline & basil

serves 4

2 tablespoons olive oil

1 onion, peeled and chopped

1 garlic clove, peeled and crushed

1kg or 2lb 4oz fresh tomatoes, skinned and roughly chopped

600ml or 20fl oz vegetable stock

55g or about 2oz farfalline or other small pasta shapes

salt and freshly ground black pepper

fresh basil leaves, to serve

1 Heat the oil in a large saucepan, put in the onion and garlic, stir briefly, then cover and leave to cook gently for ten minutes, until the onions start to become soft.

2 Add the tomatoes, stir, then cover and cook for a further ten to fifteen minutes, until the tomatoes have collapsed.

3 Add the stock, bring to the boil, then lower the heat and leave to simmer for five minutes, Then put in the farfalline and cook for a further five to eight minutes.

4 Season the soup to taste, then serve it into warm bowls. Tear some fresh basil leaves over each one as a garnish.

A man taking basil from a woman will love her always.

Sir Thomas Moore

chilled red pepper soup

This vibrant soup is also good hot – very useful if the weather changes.

4 large red peppers, deseeded,
  roughly chopped

2 fat garlic cloves, no need to peel

½ teaspoon vegetarian bouillon powder

squeeze of lemon juice

basil leaves or a little chopped avocado,
  to garnish

1 Simmer the red peppers and garlic in a little water until very tender. Purée in a food processor, then sieve.

2 Return the mixture to the saucepan along with the bouillon powder and enough water to make the consistency you like, but don't make it too thin, as it's naturally very light in texture.

3 Add a dash of lemon juice and salt and pepper to taste. Chill.

4 Serve in icy bowls, topped with torn basil leaves and (or) diced avocado.

Who for such dainties would not stoop?
Soup of the evening, beautiful soup!

Lewis Carroll
'The Mock Turtle's Song'

egyptian lentil soup

2 tablespoons olive oil

2 large onions, peeled and chopped

6 garlic cloves, sliced

250g or 9oz split red lentils

2 celery sticks

1 bay leaf

½ teaspoon turmeric

1.2 litres or 40fl oz water

2 teaspoons ground cumin

2 teaspoons ground coriander

juice of 1 lemon

salt and pepper

1 Heat one tablespoonful of the olive oil in a large saucepan or pressure-cooker. Add half the onions and fry gently for seven to ten minutes, until they are beginning to soften.

2 Add half the garlic, the lentils, celery, bay leaf and turmeric to the pan. Stir, then add the water. Bring to the boil then cook for five minutes on high pressure in a pressure-cooker or simmer, covered, for fifteen minutes, until the lentils are tender.

3 Meanwhile, fry the remaining onion in the rest of the olive oil, for about ten minutes, or until soft. Stir in the rest of the garlic, the cumin and coriander, cook for a minute or two until the spices smell aromatic, then remove from the heat.

4 Remove the bay leaf from the soup and discard. Whizz the soup in a food-processor or blender until smooth. Add more water if you'd rather have a thinner consistency.

5 Stir in the lemon juice, salt and freshly ground black pepper to taste, then swirl in the onion and spice mixture – or top each bowlful with it.

flageolet bean
& avocado salad

serves 4

2 x 400g or 14oz cans flageolet beans,
   drained and rinsed

3 tablespoons olive oil

1 tablespoon red-wine vinegar

salt and coarsely ground black pepper

2 ripe avocados

squeeze of fresh lemon juice

3–4 tablespoons chopped summer herbs:
   parsley, chives, mint, chervil...
   whatever is available

1 Put the beans into a mixing bowl with the olive oil, vinegar and a grinding of black pepper and mix gently.

2 Just before serving the salad, peel and slice the avocados and toss the pieces in lemon juice. Season with salt and pepper.

3 Gently stir the avocado into the bean salad, along with the herbs and serve soon. This is lovely with a summer salad of sliced tomatoes, onions and black olives.

Condiments are like old friends: highly thought of, but often taken for granted.

Marilyn Kaytor
Look Magazine, 1963

summer tomato salad

Such a lovely salad that seems to go with just about everything.

serves 4

450g or 1lb tomatoes

1 teaspoon balsamic vinegar

2 tablespoons olive oil

salt and freshly ground black pepper

1 mild onion, finely chopped, optional

handful of black olives, optional

torn basil leaves

1 Slice the tomatoes, discarding any hard pieces of core. Put them into a shallow bowl and sprinkle with balsamic vinegar, the olive oil and salt and pepper to taste.

2 Add the onion and olives, if you're using these. Leave to marinate for anything from thirty minutes to two hours, stirring from time to time.

3 Just before serving, sprinkle with torn basil leaves.

It's difficult to think anything but pleasant thoughts while eating a home-grown tomato.
Louis Grizzard

warm new potato, cherry tomato & asparagus salad

Delectable when made in early summer with Jersey Royal potatoes, the first of the season's asparagus, and tiny, sweet cherry tomatoes. Serve as a side dish or as a light meal with soft, creamy cheese, such as peppered Boursin, or perhaps goats cheese.

serves 4

500g or 1lb 2oz Jersey Royal or other new potatoes, washed

225–250g or 8–9oz bunch of asparagus

225–250g or 8–9oz cherry tomatoes, halved

2 tablespoons freshly squeezed lemon juice

1 tablespoon olive oil

4 tablespoons roughly torn basil

salt and freshly ground black pepper

1 The potatoes need to be roughly the same size, so halve or quarter as necessary. Put into a saucepan, cover with water, bring to the boil, cover and leave them to simmer for about ten minutes, or until the potatoes are almost cooked.

2 Bend the asparagus until the hard, tough ends break off. Discard these. Wash the asparagus carefully, as it can harbour grit in the flower heads. Cut each spear into two or three pieces, discarding the flower heads.

3 Add the stems of the asparagus to the pan of potatoes. Let them boil for a couple of minutes, then add the rest of the asparagus and cook for a few more minutes, or until both the asparagus and the potatoes are tender but not at all soggy when pierced with a sharp knife.

4 Drain. Add the cherry tomatoes, lemon juice, olive oil, basil and salt and pepper to taste. Toss the salad and serve it hot or warm. It also tastes great cold.

easy greek salad
with warm pitta bread

Bring back summer with this easy salad.

serves 4

2–4 pitta breads

200g or 7oz feta cheese

450g or 1lb tomatoes

½ cucumber, peeled

2 large spring onions

juice of half a lemon

1 teaspoon white-wine vinegar or cider vinegar

1 handful of black olives

2 tablespoons olive oil

freshly ground black pepper

1 Warm the pitta breads under the grill.

2 Meanwhile, slice the cheese, the tomatoes and the cucumber into even-sized pieces. Slice the spring onions. Put all of these into a bowl with the lemon juice, vinegar, olives and oil.

3 Grind in a bit of pepper, toss gently and serve with warm bread.

My dear, I love you ardently
Adore your charm, the way you look,
I'm captivated by your voice,
I've read with pride your latest book,
And yet I will not marry you
Until, sweetheart, you've learned to cook.

Martyno
'Ultimatum'

warm sweet potato salad

serves 2

2 red-fleshed sweet potatoes, scrubbed

1 tablespoon olive oil

200g or 7oz feta cheese

1 bunch or packet of watercress, washed

1 handful of black olives

salt and freshly ground black pepper

The potato, like man, was not meant to dwell alone.

Shila Hibben

1 Preheat the oven to 200°C (400°F or gas mark 6).

2 Cut the sweet potatoes into 1cm (half-inch) squares. Place these in a roasting tin with the oil and mix thoroughly. Bake for thirty minutes, until tender and lightly browned.

3 Cut the cheese into cubes roughly the same size as the sweet-potato squares.

4 Put the watercress into a salad bowl then add the hot sweet potatoes, cheese and olives. Season with a little salt and pepper (not too much salt, because of the saltiness of the feta) and serve. The sharpness of the feta cheese and saltiness of the olives contrast perfectly with the sweetness of the potatoes.

baby spinach & summer berry salad

Thanks to my friend Annie for this delicious and unusual salad, which she kept raving about. She insisted, so I tried it. Then I began to rave, too.

serves 2–4

1 tablespoon raspberry vinegar

2 tablespoons olive oil

salt and freshly ground black pepper

1 red onion, finely sliced

100g or 3½oz flaked almonds

225g or 8oz firm log goats cheese

1 packet baby leaf spinach

225g or 8oz summer berries: raspberries, strawberries or blueberries, ready to eat

1 Mix the raspberry vinegar, olive oil and some salt and pepper in a salad bowl. Add the onion and leave on one side. This can be done in advance if convenient, which allows the onion to soften in the dressing, but it is not essential.

2 Put the flaked almonds in a dry saucepan, stir over the heat for a few minutes until they turn golden, then tip them onto a plate before they overcook.

3 Cut the goats cheese into bite-size pieces, and grill until nicely browned.

4 Mix the spinach, berries and almonds into the salad bowl, then top with the hot goats cheese and serve at once.

Eat, laugh and enjoy the earth
And feed your love for all it's worth.

Anonymous

a vegetarian caesar

Everyone loves Caesar salad, but if you're vegetarian, you've almost always got to make it yourself, as the restaurant versions usually contain anchovies. It's easy to do; just replace fishy flavours with zingy ingredients such as Tabasco and capers, and make gorgeous generous-sized croûtons as well.

serves 2–4

1 small, slim baguette or ficelle

olive oil

4 tablespoons good-quality mayonnaise

1 garlic clove, crushed

Tabasco sauce

2 tablespoons capers, rinsed and drained

125g or 4oz fresh Parmesan, grated

1 cos lettuce, washed

1 Heat the grill. Cut the baguette into slices about 5mm (a quarter of an inch) thick. Brush both sides with olive oil and grill until golden on both sides, turning them over when the first side is done.

2 Meanwhile, mix the mayonnaise with the garlic and add some Tabasco sauce; shake some drops in, then taste to get the right heat. Stir in the capers and half the cheese.

3 Tear the lettuce into rough, largish pieces and put them all into a salad bowl. Add the mayonnaise mixture, the croutons and the remaining Parmesan, mix gently, and serve.

To make a good salad is to be a brilliant diplomatist. The problem is entirely the same in both cases: to know how much oil one must mix with one's vinegar.

Oscar Wilde

pasta salad with fennel, tomatoes & olives

This salad is dressed with a mixture of mayonnaise and yogurt for a less fatty result. This is great served with some warm crusty bread.

serves 4

400g or 14oz conchiglie

salt to taste

3 tablespoons olive oil

1 tablespoon wine vinegar (white or red)

½ teaspoon Dijon mustard

1 garlic clove peeled and crushed

freshly ground black pepper

1 large fennel bulb

450g or 1lb tomatoes, preferably plum,
    roughly chopped

125g or 4oz black olives

1 Fill a large saucepan with four litres (seven pints) of water and put on to heat for the pasta.

2 When the water boils, add the pasta along with a teaspoon of salt and stir. Cover until the water has come back to the boil, then let the pasta bubble away, uncovered, for about eight minutes, or until it is tender but still has some bite.

3 Make a vinaigrette by putting the oil, vinegar, mustard, garlic and salt and pepper into a jar and shaking until combined.

4 Cut any leafy bits off the fennel, chop them roughly and leave them on one side. With a sharp knife, pare away any tough, stringy outer layers, then dice or chop the flesh.

5 Drain the pasta, then put it back into the still-warm pan. Add the fennel, tomatoes and olives. Give the vinaigrette a quick shake, then add to the pasta and stir gently until everything is coated. Scatter the reserved leafy bits of fennel on top. Serve immediately, or cover and leave until the salad cools to room temperature.

farfalle salad with gruyère, cherry tomatoes & spring onions

serves 4

bunch of spring onions, trimmed and cut into long ribbons

400g or 14oz farfalle

salt to taste

3 tablespoons olive oil

1 tablespoon wine vinegar (white or red)

½ teaspoon Dijon mustard

freshly ground black pepper

225g or 8oz cherry tomatoes, halved

125g or 4oz Gruyère cheese, diced or coarsely grated

2 tablespoons freshly chopped or torn flat-leaf parsley

1 Fill a large saucepan with four litres or seven pints of water and put it on the stove to heat for the pasta.

2 Meanwhile, put the spring onion ribbons into icy-cold water and leave on one side to curl.

3 When the water in the saucepan boils, add the pasta along with a teaspoon of salt and give it a quick stir. Briefly put the lid on until it starts to lift, showing that the water has come back to the boil, then let the pasta bubble away, uncovered, for about eight minutes, or until it is tender but still has some bite.

4 Make a vinaigrette by putting the oil, vinegar, mustard and a seasoning of salt and pepper into a jar and shaking until thoroughly combined.

5 Drain the pasta by tipping it all into a colander placed in the sink, then put it back into the still-warm pan. Drain the spring onions and add them to the pasta along with the tomatoes, Gruyère and parsley. Give the vinaigrette a quick shake, then add to the pasta and stir gently until everything is coated. Serve immediately, or cover and leave until the salad cools to room temperature

penne salad with radicchio, red pepper & black olives

A lovely salad, with sweet, succulent grilled red peppers contrasting with bitter-tasting radicchio leaves and salty black olives.

serves 4

2 red peppers

400g or 14oz penne

salt to taste

3 tablespoons olive oil

1 tablespoon wine vinegar (white or red)

½ teaspoon Dijon mustard

1 garlic clove, peeled and crushed

freshly ground black pepper

1 small radicchio, shredded or torn

125g or 4oz black olives

1 Fill a large saucepan with four litres or seven pints of water and put it on the stove to heat for the pasta.

2 Next, prepare the peppers by cutting them into quarters and placing skin-side (shiny side) up on a grill pan. Put under a high heat for ten to fifteen minutes, or until the skin has begun to blister and blacken in places. Cover with a plate and leave until cool enough to handle, then remove the skin, stem and seeds, and cut the flesh into strips.

3 When the water in the saucepan boils, add the pasta along with a teaspoon of salt and stir. Cover until the water has come back to the boil, then let the pasta bubble away, uncovered, for about eight minutes, or until it is tender but still has some bite.

4 Make a vinaigrette by putting the oil, vinegar, mustard, garlic and a seasoning of salt and pepper into a jar and shaking until combined.

5 Drain the pasta, then put it back into the still-warm pan. Add the red pepper strips, radicchio and olives. Give the vinaigrette a shake, then add to the pasta and stir gently until everything is well-coated. Serve immediately, or cover until the salad cools.

fig, rocket &
pine nut salad

serves 2–4

1 tablespoon balsamic vinegar

3 tablespoons olive oil

4 fresh figs, sliced

55g or 2oz pine nuts, toasted

2 packets or handfuls of rocket

salt and freshly ground black pepper

1 Put the vinegar and olive oil into a salad bowl with
a good seasoning of salt and pepper. Add the figs,
pine nuts and rocket and toss gently.

2 Serve at once. This is delicious with some soft goats
cheese and rye bread.

watermelon, feta, olive & mint salad

serves 4

200g or 7oz feta, cut into cubes

450g or 1lb peeled and deseeded watermelon, cut into cubes

125g or 4oz black or green olives

handful of mint leaves

olive oil, optional

balsamic vinegar, optional

salt and freshly ground black pepper, to taste

Simply mix the first four ingredients together in a salad bowl. It's very good just as it is, but you could dress it lightly by adding one to two tablespoons olive oil and a few drops of vinegar to the bowl, and a little salt and pepper.

veggie salade niçoise

250g or 9oz fine green beans,
   trimmed as necessary

1 tablespoon red-wine vinegar

3 tablespoons olive oil

½ teaspoon Dijon mustard

1 garlic clove, crushed

4 tomatoes, sliced

125g or 4oz black olives

1 mild onion, thinly sliced

4 hard-boiled eggs, quartered, optional

several sprigs of basil, torn

salt and freshly ground black pepper

1 Cook the beans in a little fast-boiling water until they're just tender – around three to six minutes, depending on their thickness. Drain.

2 Mix the vinegar, olive oil, Dijon mustard, garlic and a good seasoning of salt and pepper in a salad bowl.

3 Add the hot beans and all the other ingredients, then toss lightly.

4 Serve at once. This is delicious with some soft goats cheese and rye bread.

One cannot think well, love well, sleep well, if one has not dined well.

Virginia Woolf

goats cheese & sun-dried tomato salad

serves 4

1 tablespoon red-wine vinegar

3 tablespoons olive oil

½ teaspoon Dijon mustard

1 garlic clove, crushed

1 large summer lettuce (oak-leaf or loose-head type), torn into pieces

8 sun-dried tomatoes in oil, drained and chopped

55g or 2oz walnut pieces, toasted

55g or 2oz raisins

2 tablespoons chopped chives

2 x 125g or 4oz circles of goats cheese, roughly crumbled

salt and freshly ground black pepper

1 Mix the vinegar, olive oil, Dijon mustard, garlic and a good seasoning of salt and pepper in a large salad bowl.

2 Add the lettuce, sun-dried tomatoes, walnuts, raisins, chives and goats cheese and toss gently.

A number of rare or newly experienced foods have been claimed to be aphrodisiacs. At one time this quality was even ascribed to the tomato. Reflect on that when you are next preparing the family salad.

Jane Grigson

*Strange to see how a good dinner and
feasting reconciles everybody.*

Samuel Pepys

3

al fresco feasts

Eating outside: who can resist it? I certainly can't. I'm out there from the first golden glint of spring sunshine to the very last, long-shadowed day of Indian summer. It has been said before, but it's true: fresh air really does add something to the flavour and pleasure of food. Perhaps it's to do with the relaxation and freedom of eating *al fresco*, when fingers are as good as forks and no one's worrying about table manners. In any case, the recipes in this section are perfect for dining outside, whether you're barbecuing, picnicking – or simply eating on the patio.

red & gold peppers stuffed with feta & cherry tomatoes

serves 4

2 red peppers

2 gold peppers

450g or 1lb feta cheese, diced

125g or 4oz cherry tomatoes, halved

salt and freshly ground black pepper

1 Preheat the oven to 200°C (400°F or gas mark 6).

2 Cut the peppers in half through their stalks, then remove the seeds, leaving the stalks intact. Put them into a roasting tin or casserole dish.

3 Divide the feta cheese and cherry tomatoes equally into the pepper halves, and grind some pepper over. You could add a touch of salt, but the feta will supply lots.

4 Put into the oven and bake for about forty minutes, or until the feta is golden brown and melting, and the peppers are browning a bit at the edges.

Show me another pleasure like dinner which
comes every day and lasts an hour.
Charles Maurice de Talleyrand

leek lattice flan

serves 6

225g or 8oz shortcrust pastry

3 tablespoons oil

8 thin leeks, washed and trimmed

salt and pepper, to taste

300ml or 10fl oz sour cream

2 egg yolks

1 tablespoon chopped parsley

Eat leeks in tide and garlic in May,
and all the year after physicians may play.

Russian proverb

1 Preheat the oven to 200°C (400°F or gas mark 6).

2 Roll out the pastry and use it to line a 20cm (eight-inch) flan tin; prick the base with a fork. Cut any trimmings into long strips and wrap in foil. Bake at the top of the oven for twenty minutes.

3 Trim the leeks to fit the flan, then cook them whole in boiling salted water until tender – about fifteen to twenty minutes. Drain, then arrange them side by side in the flan case and season to taste.

4 Whisk the sour cream with the egg yolks, parsley and seasoning, then pour over the leeks. Arrange the reserved pastry strips in a lattice design over the top.

5 Reduce the oven temperature to 190°C (375°F or gas mark 5). Bake the flan in the centre of the oven for thirty-five to forty minutes, or until set.

mediterranean roast veg with halloumi

Halloumi cheese is available from most large supermarkets and makes a particularly attractive topping. Serve this on its own or with some watercress on the side.

serves 3–4

2 large baking potatoes, scrubbed

2 large red onions, peeled

2 red peppers, deseeded

2 large carrots, scrubbed

3–4 tablespoons olive oil

salt and freshly ground black pepper

5–6 garlic cloves, peeled and chopped

5–6 sprigs of rosemary, chopped

250g or 9oz halloumi cheese

1 Preheat the oven to 200°C (400°F or gas mark 6).

2 Cut the potatoes into 1cm (half-inch) squares and the rest of the vegetables into 2.5cm (one-inch) squares. Place them all in a roasting tin, then add the oil and some salt and pepper, and move the vegetables around with your hands so that they're all coated in oil.

3 Put into the oven and bake for thirty minutes. Remove from the oven, stir in the garlic and rosemary, then return to the oven for a further fifteen minutes.

4 Drain the halloumi well. Using a sharp knife, slice it as thinly as you can.

5 Remove the roasting tin of vegetables from the oven and put the slices of halloumi all over the top, then bake for a further fifteen minutes, until the halloumi is golden brown. Serve at once.

farinata

*This is a kind of polenta cake make from chickpea flour
and is a popular traditional dish in the south of France.*

serves 2-4

225g or 8oz chickpea flour

1½ teaspoons salt

1 teaspoon cumin seeds

400ml or 14fl oz cold water

6 tablespoons olive oil

freshly ground black pepper

*Cuisine is only about making foods taste the
way they are supposed to taste.*

Charlie Trotter

1 Preheat the oven to 220°C (425°F or gas mark 7).

2 Put the chickpea flour, salt and cumin seeds into a bowl and pour in enough of the water to make a creamy batter. Stir well to get rid of as many lumps as you can, then add the rest of the water. Don't worry too much about the odd lump here and there.

3 Spoon the olive oil onto a 28 x 18cm (11 x 7 inch) Swiss roll tin, then pour the batter on top of the oil. With a spoon, mix the batter and oil together as well as you can, then put it into the oven and bake for fifteen to twenty minutes, or until the top is browned and oily looking and the sides have shrunk away from the tin.

4 Serve in slices, hot, warm or cold. A tomato salad goes well with this, and it could also be served with roasted vegetables cooked in the same oven.

savoury olive mushroom cake

If you haven't any leftover white wine, water will do.
Serve in thick wedges, like a cake, with a green salad.

serves 4

300g or 10½oz self-raising 85% wholewheat flour

a pinch of salt

4 eggs

150ml or 5fl oz white wine

4 tablespoons olive oil

225g or 8oz pitted green olives, sliced

175g or 6oz mushrooms, sliced

175g or 6oz cheese, grated

butter, for greasing

to garnish
chicory
watercress

1 Preheat the oven to 250°C (500°F, or gas mark 9). Grease a 20cm or eight-inch cake or 900g (2lb) loaf tin.

2 Put the flour and salt into a mixing bowl and break in the eggs. Add the white wine and oil. Mix until smooth, then stir in the olives, the mushrooms and the cheese.

3 Spoon the mixture into the prepared tin. Bake for ten minutes, then turn down the oven to 190°C, (375°F or gas mark 5) and bake for a further forty to fifty minutes, or until firm, golden-brown and shrunk from the sides of the tin. Garnish with chicory and watercress and serve immediately.

An egg is always an adventure; the next one may be different.

Oscar Wilde

spanikopita

A Greek pie that is equally good as a starter or main course.

serves 6 as a main course,
8 as a first course
10 sheets filo pastry

150–175g or 5½–6oz butter, melted

900g or 2lb fresh spinach (450g or 1lb frozen
    spinach, cooked, drained and cooled)

1 bunch spring onions, trimmed and chopped

100g or 3½oz feta cheese, crumbled

salt and freshly ground black pepper

butter, for greasing

1 Preheat the oven to 200°C (400°F, or gas mark 6).

2 Grease a deep pie dish, then place a sheet of filo pastry in it, allowing the edges to hang over the sides of the dish.

3 Brush with melted butter, then place another sheet of filo pastry on top. Continue in this way, using five sheets of filo pastry. (Keep the rest covered with a damp cloth.)

4 Chop the spinach and mix with the spring onions, cheese and salt and pepper to taste. Spoon on top of the pastry.

5 Cover with the rest of the filo pastry sheets, brushing each one with butter as before, and finishing with melted butter. Neaten the sides; prick and decorate the top with leaves cut from pastry trimmings.

6 Bake for forty to forty-five minutes. Serve either hot or warm.

onion & sour cream flan

serves 4–6

175g or 6oz shortcrust pastry

2 tablespoons oil

350g or 12oz onions, peeled and sliced

25g or 1oz butter

150ml or 5fl oz sour cream

2 egg yolks

salt and pepper

grated nutmeg

There is in every cook's opinion
No savoury dish without an onion.
But lest your kissing should be spoiled,
The onion must be thoroughly boiled.

Jonathan Swift

1 Preheat the oven to 200°C (400°F or gas mark 6).

2 Roll out the pastry and use it to line a 20cm (eight-inch) flan tin; prick the base with a fork. Bake at the top of the oven for twenty minutes.

3 Meanwhile, heat the oil in a small saucepan, and as soon as the flan case is ready, pour the hot oil onto the base; leave to one side.

4 Fry the onion in the butter until softened – around ten minutes. Cool slightly, then add the cream, egg yolks, seasoning and nutmeg. Stir well and pour into the flan case.

5 Reduce the oven temperature to 180°C (350°F or gas mark 4). Bake the flan in the centre of the oven for thirty-five to forty minutes, or until set.

courgettes with onions, pine nuts & raisins

Serve this hot, warm or cold, as a tapas, first course or salad. To turn it into more of a meal, have it with some hot, fluffy couscous.

serves 4

2 good-sized courgettes: 225g or 8oz each, cut into 1cm or ½-inch dice

sea salt and black pepper

1 tablespoon olive oil

1 large purple onion, fairly finely sliced

small handful of raisins

small handful of pine nuts, toasted

1 Put the courgettes into a colander and sprinkle with salt. This will draw out some of their water so they'll stay crisp.

2 Heat the oil in a large saucepan, put in the onion, cover and cook gently for twenty minutes, until it's sweet and tender, stirring often.

3 Blot the courgettes on kitchen paper and add to the onion with the raisins. Cover again and cook for a further seven to ten minutes, until the courgette is tender and the raisins plump. Stir in the pine nuts and salt and pepper to taste.

The true cook is the perfect blend – the only perfect blend – of artist and philosopher.

Norman Douglas

roasted mediterranean vegetables

serves 4

2 red peppers, deseeded and chopped

2 aubergines, cut into chunks

3 red onions, cut into chunks

2 courgettes, sliced

4 plum tomatoes, halved

8 garlic cloves, peeled

4 tablespoons olive oil

3 sprigs of thyme

salt and freshly ground black pepper

1 Preheat the oven to 220°C (425°F, gas mark 7). Put all the vegetables into a roasting tin, pour over the olive oil; make sure all vegetables are well-coated.

2 Add the thyme, salt and pepper, then put into the oven and roast for thirty-five to forty minutes, or until the vegetables are tender, stirring occasionally.

grilled asparagus with lemon marinade

serves 2–4

450g or 1lb asparagus, washed and trimmed

for the marinade
6 tablespoons olive oil

100ml or 3½oz white wine

grated rind and juice of 1 lemon

1 garlic clove, crushed

½ teaspoon sea salt

1 bay leaf, torn in half

1 teaspoon coarsely crushed black peppercorns

1 Mix the marinade ingredients together. Then, place the asparagus in a shallow dish and pour on the marinade, turning the veg to coat. Cover and leave for thirty to forty-five minutes.

2 Drain off excess marinade; reserve. Barbecue or grill the asparagus for ten minutes, or until just tender, turning as needed. Pour on the reserved marinade to serve.

grilled polenta with spicy dipping sauce

1.2 litres or 40fl oz water

225g or 8oz polenta

125g or 4oz Parmesan, grated

125g or 4oz pitted olives, sliced, optional

salt and freshly ground black pepper

olive oil, for brushing

for the sauce
1 onion, finely chopped

1 tablespoon olive oil

2 garlic cloves, chopped

400g or 14oz can chopped tomatoes

½ teaspoon red chilli flakes

dash of honey

1 First, make the sauce by frying the onion in the oil in a saucepan until tender – around seven to ten minutes. Stir in the garlic, then add the tomatoes and chilli flakes and simmer for about fifteen minutes, or until all the extra liquid has gone.

2 Purée in a blender or food processor if you want a smooth texture. Season with salt, pepper and a dash of honey and set aside.

3 Put the water into a large saucepan and bring to the boil. Add the polenta in a thin, steady stream, stirring all the time. Simmer for five to ten minutes, or until it's very thick and leaves the sides of the pan, stirring occasionally.

4 Remove from the heat; stir in the cheese and salt and pepper to taste. Turn onto a lightly oiled baking sheet or large plate; press out to a depth of 5–8mm (¼ –⅜ inch). Leave until completely cold and firm.

5 Just before serving, heat a griddle, grill or barbecue. Cut the polenta into small pieces, brush lightly with oil and grill on both sides until crisp and lightly charred. Serve at once, with the sauce.

garlic mushroom skewers

makes 8 skewers

24 button mushrooms, or about 48 mixed
   wild mushrooms, if available

for the marinade

6 tablespoons olive oil

6–8 garlic cloves, crushed

juice of 3 lemons

freshly milled black pepper

8 skewers, wooden ones soaked in water for
   30 minutes to prevent burning

*Nature alone is antique, and the oldest art
a mushroom.*

Thomas Carlyle

1 First, mix all the marinade ingredients together.

2 Wash the mushrooms carefully and pat dry on kitchen paper. Mix the mushrooms with the marinade, ensuring that they are all well-coated. Leave for at least thirty minutes, then thread the mushrooms onto the skewers, shaking off and keeping any excess marinade.

3 Cook the skewers on the barbecue or under a hot grill for about ten minutes, until the mushrooms are cooked through and browned all over. Baste with any excess marinade as necessary during the cooking time and spoon any remaining over the mushrooms before serving.

4 Serve with soft bread or baps.

braised summer carrots

These are gorgeous – meltingly tender to eat and so easy to do. Serve them with a cooked grain dish and some hummus for a simple, balanced meal.

serves 4

500g or 1lb 2oz carrots

1 tablespoon olive oil

2 large garlic cloves, sliced

1 tablespoon lemon juice or cider vinegar

150ml or 5fl oz water

sea salt and freshly ground black pepper

chopped flat-leaf parsley

1 Scrub the carrots if they're organic, otherwise peel, top and tail. Slice them quite thinly – about as thick as pound coins.

2 Heat the olive oil in a pan; put in the carrots and stir for two to three minutes to bring out the flavour.

3 Add the garlic, lemon juice or vinegar, water, a pinch of salt and a grinding of pepper.

4 Bring to the boil, then turn the heat down low and leave them to simmer gently for twenty minutes, or until they are meltingly tender – offering no resistance when pierced with the point of a knife – and bathed in just a little glossy liquid.

5 Scatter the parsley on top and serve.

Serenely full, the epicure would say,
Fate cannot harm me, I have dined today.

Sydney Smith
in *Lady Holland's Memoir*

grilled halloumi cheese

Halloumi doesn't melt when heated, so it's perfect for the barbecue. Cut and skewer it or cook it flat on the grill, like a burger – this way it gets delectably browned and charred. It's inclined to dry out, so needs to be brushed with oil. Better still, soak it in a marinade for thirty minutes before cooking.

serves 4
2 x 250g packets of halloumi cheese

for the marinade
6 tablespoons olive oil

100ml or 3½oz white wine

grated rind and juice of 1 lemon

1 garlic clove, crushed

½ teaspoon sea salt

1 bay leaf, torn in half

1 teaspoon coarsely crushed black peppercorns

1 Mix all the marinade ingredients together.

2 Drain the liquid in which the halloumi is packed and blot with kitchen paper. Cut into slices about 5mm (a quarter-inch) thick; you will get about eight slices from each packet.

3 Put the slices into a shallow dish, cover with the marinade and leave for about thirty minutes.

4 To grill or barbecue, first drain off and reserve the excess marinade. Place the pieces of cheese on the barbecue or under a grill and cook until browned on one side, then turn over to do the other side. It takes about three to four minutes to cook each side. This is nicest when well-browned and crisp.

5 Serve with any remaining marinade poured over.

Many's the long night I've dreamed of cheese
– toasted, mostly.

Robert Louis Stevenson

homemade lemonade

serves 4–6
5 large lemons, preferably organic, unwaxed

750ml or 27fl oz water

100–200g (3½–7oz) granulated sugar

To serve
ice cubes

extra water, still or fizzy, chilled

any of the following: sprigs of fresh mint,
    borage flowers, a dash of lemon liqueur

*We are living in a world today where
lemonade is made from artificial flavors
and furniture polish is made from real lemons.*
                                        Alfred E. Newman

1 Scrub the lemons, then grate the rind from three of them, using a fine grater or zester – be careful not to get any of the white pith, because that could give the lemonade a bitter taste.

2 Put the zest into a large bowl or jug. Squeeze the juice from all the lemons and add to the jug, along with the water and the smaller quantity of sugar.

3 Stir and chill. This becomes better the longer it stands; overnight is fine. Add some more sugar to taste, if necessary, then strain the lemonade into a serving jug.

4 You can serve it as it is, with ice-cubes, and some extra cold water (still or fizzy, as you like, if required) sprigs of fresh mint and borage flowers and a dash of lemon liqueur if you want to give it an extra kick.

iced tea

serves 4–6

1.2 litres or 42fl oz fresh cold water

4 tea bags Ceylon or English breakfast tea

1–2 tablespoons caster sugar

To serve
ice-cubes

sprigs of fresh mint

any, or all, of the following: orange, lemon
    and lime slices

½ lime, sliced

1 Bring 400ml (14fl oz) of the water to the boil.

2 Put the tea bags into a bowl and pour the water over them. Cover and leave to steep for twenty to thirty minutes, then squeeze the tea bags to extract all the flavour, and discard.

3 Add the remaining 800ml (28fl oz) of cold water to the tea. Sweeten to taste with the sugar. Cover and refrigerate until ready to serve.

4 Serve the tea in tall glasses, or pour from a glass jug, with plenty of ice, sprigs of fresh mint and orange, lemon and lime slices as desired.

Iced tea is too pure and natural a creation not to have been invented as soon as tea, ice, and hot weather crossed paths.

John Egerton

chufa nut milk

This is delicious chilled as a drink or poured over cereal, fruit or puddings – a great choice for anyone trying to avoid dairy products.

serves 4–6

250g or 9oz chufa or tiger nuts

1 litre or 35fl oz water

1 Wash the chufa or tiger nuts, then liquidize them with the water in a blender or food processor.

2 Leave to stand for three to four hours, then strain and use as milk.

mint tea

serves 4–6

6 teaspoons or tea bags pure green tea

a good handful of fresh mint leaves

1 litre or 35fl oz boiling water

55g or 2oz granulated sugar

1 Put the tea and mint leaves into a teapot and pour on the boiling water. In Morocco, the sugar is also added to the pot. I don't like sweet mint tea, so I leave this out and let people sweeten it themselves.

2 Let it steep for two minutes – green tea doesn't need as long as black tea – then add more water and sugar to taste.

3 Pour into individual cups – glass ones are traditional – and serve.

sangria

The Med wouldn't be the Med without sangria. There are zillions of versions, so there are no hard and fast rules as far as recipes go. The key is to start with Rioja and fruit, then add fruit juices, liqueur, ice, fizzy water, lemonade, etc, and mix it all up to your own taste.

serves 6

1 bottle Rioja

small glass Grand Marnier or other orange liqueur

2 oranges, sliced

1 lemon, sliced

1 lime, sliced

ice-cubes

soda water, to taste

6 strawberries, halved

mint leaves

1 Mix the wine, Grand Marnier, oranges, lemon and lime in a large jug and set aside – it can easily stand for two to three hours or more for the flavours to develop fully.

2 To serve, pour over ice, top up with soda water as required and decorate with strawberries and some mint leaves.

Just a perfect day
drink Sangria in the park...

Lou Reed
'Perfect Day'

*Ponder well on this point: the pleasant hours
of our life are all connected by a more or less
tangible link, with some memory of the table.*
Charles Pierre Monselet

sunny snacks
& suppers

You can feel the Mediterranean sunshine in these recipes: roasted peppers with tomato filling from Italy, or with spicy raisins and pine nut filling from Greece; Summer Pepper Stew with Parmesan Toasts from Provence; Middle-Eastern Bulgur Wheat Pilaf; Turkish Aubergine Pilaf; Penne with Grilled Mediterranean Vegetables, or with mint pesto, peas and broad beans; Oven-baked Ratatouille, some creamy French flans... All of them make perfect summer food, but are also guaranteed to brighten up the darkest day. Make some, and let them brighten your mood with their warmth and flavour – wherever you are, whatever the weather.

piedmontese peppers

*So quick and easy – and you can make them into a
complete meal by serving with some couscous, a
green salad and maybe a dollop of hummus.*

serves 2

2 red peppers

2 tomatoes, chopped

8 black olives

2 garlic cloves, chopped

1 tablespoon capers

4 teaspoons olive oil

2 teaspoons balsamic vinegar

salt and freshly ground black pepper

1 Preheat the oven to 200°C (400°F or gas mark 6).

2 Halve the peppers through their stems, leaving them intact. Cut away the white cores and rinse away the seeds under the tap.

3 Put the peppers, cut-side up, in a roasting tin. Divide the tomatoes, olives, garlic and capers among them, then drizzle the olive oil and balsamic vinegar on top and season with the salt and pepper.

4 Bake for about thirty minutes, or until the peppers are tender and just beginning to brown around the edges.

Cooking is at once child's play and adult joy.
And, cooking done with care is an act of love.
Craig Clairborne

red peppers with raisin & pine nut stuffing

serves 4

125g or 4oz Basmati rice

2 tablespoons olive oil

2 onions, chopped

2 garlic cloves, chopped

4 red peppers

½ teaspoon cinnamon

125g or 4oz raisins

4 tablespoons toasted pine nuts

4 tomatoes, chopped

Rice is a beautiful food.

Shizuo Tsuji

1 Preheat the oven to 180°C (350°F or gas mark 4).

2 Cook the rice in a panful of boiling water for ten to fifteen minutes, until tender, or following packet directions; drain.

3 Heat the olive oil in a saucepan, add the onions and garlic, cover and cook gently for ten minutes, until tender, stirring occasionally.

4 Cut the tops of the peppers to make 'lids'. Scoop out and discard the insides. If necessary, shave off a little of the bases to make them stand level.

5 Mix the rice with half the onion, the cinnamon, raisins, pine nuts and salt and pepper to taste. Pack this mixture into the red peppers and put the 'lids; on top.

6 Put the rest of the onion, the tomatoes and some salt and pepper into a deep ovenproof dish, then put the four peppers on top. Put into the oven and cook for forty-five minutes to an hour, or until the peppers are very tender and the tomatoes collapsed into a sauce. Serve with thick yogurt and a green salad.

summer pepper stew with parmesan toasts

serves 4

2 tablespoons olive oil

2 large onions, sliced

4 red peppers, cored, deseeded and sliced

4 golden peppers, cored, deseeded and sliced

4 garlic cloves, finely chopped

450g or 1lb cherry tomatoes, stems removed

20g or ¾oz basil leaves, torn

salt and pepper

for the Parmesan toasts
4 slices wholemeal or country bread

25g or 1oz butter

55g or 2oz grated Parmesan cheese

1 Heat the oil in a large saucepan, put in the onions and cook, covered, for five minutes.

2 Add the peppers and garlic, cover and cook gently for fifteen to twenty minutes, until the peppers are tender.

3 Add the tomatoes, and cook for a further ten to fifteen minutes, until they have collapsed. Season with salt and pepper, stir in the torn basil leaves and serve with the toasts.

4 To make the toasts, toast the bread under the grill on one side only. Remove from the grill, spread the untoasted side with butter, sprinkle with Parmesan and put back under the grill.

5 Grill until the cheese has melted and the bread crisped. Cut into triangles and serve with the stew.

A world without tomatoes is like a string quartet without violins.

Laurie Colwin

french lettuce, pea & spring onion flan

serves 4–6

175g or 6oz shortcrust pastry

2 tablespoons oil

6 spring onions, chopped

½ lettuce, shredded

125g or 4oz shelled fresh peas or
frozen petits pois

25g or 1oz butter

6 sprigs of mint, chopped

150ml or 5fl oz single cream or milk

1 egg yolk

salt and pepper, to taste

1 Preheat the oven to 200°C (400°F or gas mark 6).

2 Roll out the pastry and use it to line a 20cm (eight-inch) flan tin; prick the base with a fork. Bake at the top of the oven for twenty minutes.

3 Meanwhile, heat the oil in a small saucepan, and as soon as the flan case is ready, pour the hot oil onto the base; leave to one side.

4 Fry the spring onions, lettuce and peas gently in the butter for two to three minutes. Remove from the heat, mix in the mint, cream, egg and seasoning, then pour into the flan case.

5 Reduce the oven temperature to 190°C (375°F or gas mark 5). Bake for thirty to thirty-five minutes, or until set.

As for the garden of mint, the very smell of it alone recovers and refreshes our spirits...

Pliny

mushroom flan

175g or 6oz shortcrust pastry

2 tablespoons oil

1 onion, chopped

25g or 1oz butter

350g or 12oz button mushrooms,
    washed and chopped

1 small garlic clove, crushed

300ml or 10fl oz sour or single cream

2 egg yolks

salt and pepper, to taste

grated nutmeg

1 Preheat the oven to 200°C (400°F or gas mark 6).

2 Roll out the pastry and use it to line a 20cm (eight-inch) flan tin; prick the base with a fork. Bake at the top of the oven for twenty minutes.

3 Meanwhile, heat the oil in a small saucepan, and as soon as the flan case is ready, pour the hot oil onto the base; leave to one side.

4 Fry the onion gently in the butter for five minutes, then add the mushrooms and garlic and cook until the mushrooms are tender – about five to six minutes. If the mushrooms produce liquid, continue to cook, uncovered, over a high heat until this has evaporated; this can take twenty to thirty minutes. Spoon the mushroom mixture into the flan case.

5 Whisk the cream and egg yolks, add the seasoning, nutmeg and parsley, then pour into the flan case.

6 Reduce the oven temperature to 190°C (375°F or gas mark 5). Bake for forty to forty-five minutes, until set.

bulgur wheat pilaf

This is good hot or cold, as an accompaniment to vegetable and bean dishes. If you're serving it with something spicy, you could leave out the cumin and coriander; if with something containing either nuts or dried fruit, leave these out. This can be made as simple or complex as you wish, to suit the occasion.

serves 4

300g or 10½oz bulgur wheat

1 onion, chopped

2 tablespoons olive oil

1 teaspoon ground cumin, optional

1 teaspoon ground coriander, optional

55g or 2oz pine nuts, toasted, optional

55g or 2oz raisins, optional

4 tablespoons chopped parsley

1 Put the bulgur wheat into a bowl and cover with boiling water. Leave to soak for ten to fifteen minutes, or until the wheat has swollen and softened; drain off any remaining water.

2 Meanwhile, fry the onion in the oil for ten minutes, until tender. If you're using the spices, nuts or raisins, add these to the onion and stir for one to two minutes, then add the wheat.

3 Stir until heated through, then remove from the heat and add the parsley and salt and pepper to taste.

A cook, when I dine, seems to me a divine being, who from the depths of his kitchen rules the human race. One considers him as a minister of heaven, because his kitchen is a temple, in which his ovens are the altar.

Desaugiers

egyptian rice & lentils

A wonderful, traditional Egyptian dish. For a complete meal, start with hummus and pitta bread and serve the rice and lentils with some cooked spinach.

serves 4

150g or 5½oz Puy lentils

1 bay leaf

4 onions, peeled and sliced

1 tablespoon olive oil

1½ teaspoons ground cumin

1½ teaspoons ground coriander

350g or 12oz Basmati rice

salt and freshly ground black pepper

1 Put the lentils into a saucepan with the bay leaf and water to cover them generously. Bring to the boil, then leave to simmer gently for about forty minutes, until tender.

2 Meanwhile, fry the onions gently in the oil with the cumin and coriander for fifteen to twenty minutes, or until very tender and sweet, stirring them often.

3 Cook the rice in a large pan of boiling water for twelve to fifteen minutes, or until tender but not soggy. Drain and rinse under the cold tap, then put back into the saucepan.

4 Drain the lentils as necessary, then add to the rice along with half the onion and a good seasoning of salt and pepper. Cook over a gentle heat, stirring often, for a few minutes until heated through, then serve, topped with the remaining onion.

A poem was never worth as much as a dinner.
Joseph Berchoux

turkish aubergine pilaf

serves 4

2 aubergines, sliced lengthwise

3 tablespoons olive oil

1 onion, peeled and chopped

2 large garlic cloves, sliced

2 teaspoons cumin seeds

225g or 8oz tomatoes, chopped

225g or 8oz basmati rice

400ml or 14fl oz boiling water

salt and freshly ground black pepper

juice of 1 lemon

We may live without friends;
we may live without books;
But civilized man cannot live without cooks.

Owen Meredith

1 Cut the aubergine halves into slices about 1cm (half an inch) thick again, so you have four slices from each. Use two tablespoons of the oil to brush the slices, then grill them until golden brown on both sides. Cut into pieces and set aside.

2 In a covered pan, cook the onion in the remaining oil for seven to eight minutes, stirring occasionally. Add the garlic, cumin and tomatoes. Cook uncovered for about ten minutes, until any wateriness has gone.

3 Stir the rice into the tomato mixture, along with a generous teaspoonful of salt and a grinding of pepper. Pour in the boiling water, cover and leave to cook for ten minutes.

4 Remove the pan from the heat. Pour the lemon juice on top and then put the aubergines on top of that. Cover and leave to stand, off the heat, for ten minutes.

5 Mix with a fork, taste and add more seasoning, if necessary, then serve.

chickpea &
aubergine casserole

*Wonderful hot with bulgur wheat and maybe
a dollop of yogurt. Also delicious cold with a
tomato salad and bread.*

serves 4

2 aubergines

2 onions

6 garlic cloves, peeled and chopped

1 thin-skinned organic lemon

1 red chilli

2 x 420g or 14–15oz cans chickpeas

handful of green olives, pitted

pinch of saffron threads

1 teaspoon salt

1 Preheat the oven to 200°C (400°F or gas mark 6).

2 Trim the aubergine and cut into 1cm (half-inch) pieces. Peel and chop the onions and garlic, slice the lemon thinly, deseed and slice the chilli. Put all into a deep casserole dish.

3 Add the chickpeas and their liquid to the casserole, along with the olives.

4 In a jug mix the saffron with 150ml (5fl oz) of boiling water and add a teaspoon of salt. Pour this over the vegetables in the casserole and mix well.

5 Cover and bake in the preheated oven for forty-five minutes. Stir the casserole, then return it to the oven and cook uncovered for a further thirty minutes.

One can say everything best over a meal.

George Eliot

penne with grilled mediterranean vegetables

serves 4

400g or 14oz penne

1 aubergine

1 large courgette

1 red onion

2 large garlic cloves, chopped

1 tablespoon olive oil

1 tablespoon freshly squeezed lemon juice

salt and pepper

1 red pepper, deseeded

16–20 cherry tomatoes

several sprigs fresh basil, to garnish

1 Preheat the grill to high.

2 Cut the aubergine and courgettes into strips about the size of your thumb, and cut the red onion into sixths or eighths. Put them all onto a grill pan or oven tin which will fit under your grill and add the garlic, olive oil, lemon and some salt and pepper. Turn the vegetables with a spoon or your hands until they are all coated with the oil.

3 Cut the pepper into strips about the same size as the other vegetables and add to the tin; the pepper does not need coating with the oil, as it cooks well without.

4 Place the pan under the grill and cook for about fifteen minutes, stirring often, until all the vegetables are browned at the edges. Add the tomatoes and cook for a few minutes longer.

5 Meanwhile, bring a large pan of water to the boil and put in the penne. Cook according to packet directions until *al dente*. Drain into a colander, then put back into the still-warm pan and add the grilled vegetables. Serve on warmed plates and garnish with torn basil leaves.

fusilli with young summer vegetables

serves 4

125g or 4oz baby carrots, trimmed and scrubbed

225g or 8oz asparagus, trimmed,
    cut in 1cm or ½-inch lengths

400g or 14oz fusilli

salt to taste

225g or 8oz podded fresh broad beans

125g or 4oz podded fresh peas
freshly ground black pepper

2 tablespoons olive oil

25g or 1oz butter

2 tablespoons fresh chopped chives

1 Fill a large saucepan with four litres (seven pints) of water and put it on the stove to heat for the pasta. When the water boils, add the pasta along with a teaspoon of salt and give it a quick stir. Briefly put the lid on until it starts to lift, showing that the water has come back to the boil, then let the pasta bubble away, uncovered, for about eight minutes, or until it is tender but still has some bite.

2 Meanwhile, cook the baby carrots and asparagus in a little boiling water for six to eight minutes, or until tender, adding the broad beans and fresh peas two to three minutes before the other vegetables are done. Drain and keep warm.

3 Drain the pasta by tipping it into a colander placed in the sink, then put it back into the still-warm pan with the olive oil, butter, drained vegetables, chopped herbs and salt and pepper to taste. Stir gently, then serve at once.

provençal courgette & tomato gratin

This is a favourite summer dish of mine, adapted from Elizabeth David, full of the flavours of Provence.

serves 2

1kg or 2lb 4oz courgettes, cut in
   6mm or ¼-inch slices

salt to taste

75g or about 3oz butter

1 garlic clove, crushed

2 tablespoons chopped parsley

500g or 1lb 2oz tomatoes, skinned and chopped

freshly grated black pepper

55g or 2oz fresh white breadcrumbs, slightly dried

1 Preheat the oven to 220°C (425°F or gas mark 7). Sprinkle the courgette slices with salt, place in a colander, cover with a plate and a weight and set aside for thirty minutes.

2 Melt 15g (½oz) of the remaining butter in a saucepan. Add the garlic, parsley, tomatoes and some salt and pepper. Cook gently, uncovered, for about fifteen minutes, to a thick purée. Set aside.

3 Drain, rinse and dry the courgettes, then fry them in the butter for a few minutes, until they are tender and translucent – you may need to do them in two batches, using half the butter for each.

4 Mix the courgettes with the tomato sauce, season to taste and place in a shallow casserole. Top with the crumbs and dot with the last 15g (½oz) of the butter. Bake for twenty-five to thirty minutes, or until golden and bubbling.

linguine with gorgonzola

One of the simplest and quickest pasta dishes, and wonderfully rich and tasty. Serve it with a simple leafy salad which includes some peppery leaves such as rocket or watercress.

serves 2

200g or 7oz linguine

175g or 6oz Gorgonzola cheese

25g or 1oz butter

freshly ground black pepper

1 Bring a large saucepan of water to the boil, put in the pasta and boil until *al dente*, following the packet directions. Drain and return to the pan.

2 Crumble the Gorgonzola into the pan on top of the hot pasta and add the butter; grind in some pepper. Toss the pasta gently so that it all gets coated with the melting cheese and butter. Serve at once.

People who know nothing about cheeses reel away from Camembert, Roquefort, and Stilton because the plebeian proboscis is not equipped to differentiate between the sordid and the sublime.

Harvey Day

fettucine with pecorino, cream & truffle oil

serves 2

250g or 9oz fettucine

150ml or 5fl oz double cream

125g or 4oz hard pecorino cheese, grated

3 tablespoons truffle oil

salt and freshly ground black pepper

fresh Parmesan, grated or flaked, to serve

1 Bring a large saucepan of water to the boil, put in the pasta and boil for about six to eight minutes (or according to the pasta packet instructions) until it's *al dente*.

2 Meanwhile, put the cream into a small saucepan with the pecorino and set aside.

3 Drain the pasta and return it to the pasta pan to keep warm. Add the truffle oil and toss well, seasoning with some salt and pepper.

4 Bring the cream to the boil, then pour into the pasta. Toss the pasta until it's thoroughly coated. Serve immediately with a bowl of Parmesan and a green salad.

Those who forget the pasta are condemned to reheat it.

Anonymous

penne with mint pesto, peas & broad beans

serves 2

250g or 9oz penne or other short pasta

125g or 4oz freshly shelled or frozen peas

125g or 4oz small, freshly shelled or frozen
broad beans

1 tablespoon mint, roughly chopped

salt and freshly ground black pepper

Parmesan, flaked or grated, to serve (optional)

for the mint pesto
1 small bunch of mint, stalks removed

1 garlic clove, crushed

2 tablespoons olive oil

1 Bring a large saucepan of water to the boil. Put in the pasta and boil until it's almost, but not quite, tender. Add the peas and broad beans and cook for a further two to three minutes, until the pasta is *al dente* and the peas and beans are done – they take practically no cooking. Drain and return to the pan.

2 Make the mint pesto by whizzing the mint, garlic and olive oil in a food processor until you have a green purée. Stir this into the pasta mixture, along with the roughly chopped mint, and season to taste.

3 Serve immediately, with some Parmesan scattered on top if desired.

As their savory odor drifts upward, a dreamy look will overspread your countenance, and as you taste their rare succulence, their yielding tenderness, their glorious just-off-the-vine flavor, a feeling of blissful satisfaction will literally permeate you.

Advertisement for frozen peas
The New Yorker, January 1936

spaghetti with chilli-tomato sauce & black olives

This is such a quick and easy sauce for pasta. You can make it in not much more time than it takes to open a jar – certainly by the time the water has boiled and the pasta has cooked. And it tastes so much nicer.

serves 2

2 tablespoons olive oil

1 onion, finely chopped

1 garlic clove, crushed

400g or 14oz can chopped tomatoes

¼ teaspoon dried chilli flakes

salt and freshly ground black pepper

200g or 7oz spaghetti

a handful of black olives

Parmesan cheese, flaked or grated, to serve

1 To start the sauce, cook the onion in one tablespoon of the olive oil in a covered saucepan for seven minutes, until tender but not browned, stirring from time to time. Add the garlic, tomatoes and chilli flakes and leave to simmer, uncovered, for ten to fifteen minutes, until thick. Season with salt and pepper.

2 Meanwhile, bring a large saucepan of water to the boil, put in the pasta and boil until *al dente*, following the packet directions. Drain and return to the pan; season to taste.

3 If you want to serve the sauce mixed with the pasta, add it now, along with the olives, and toss the pasta.

4 If you'd rather serve the pasta with the sauce on top, add a tablespoonful of olive oil to the pasta, toss, then serve the pasta in bowls, pour on the tomato sauce and top with some olives. Hand round the Parmesan separately.

Everything you see, I owe to spaghetti.

Sophia Loren

penne with tomato sauce & aubergines

serves 2

1 large aubergine, quartered lengthwise

3–4 tablespoons olive oil

1 onion, finely chopped

1 garlic clove, crushed

400g or 14oz can chopped tomatoes

¼ teaspoon dried chilli flakes

salt and freshly ground black pepper

250g or 9oz penne

fresh basil

freshly ground black pepper

Parmesan cheese, flaked to serve (optional)

1 Brush the aubergine quarters with olive oil, spread on a grill pan and grill until browned on both sides, turning them halfway through. Then cut the slices into smaller stumpy pieces.

2 Cook the onion in a tablespoonful of oil in a covered saucepan for seven minutes, stirring occasionally, until tender but not brown. Add the garlic, tomatoes and chilli flakes; simmer uncovered for ten to fifteen minutes, until thick. Season with salt and pepper.

3 Bring a large saucepan of water to the boil, put in the pasta and boil until *al dente*, following packet directions. Drain and return to the pan; season.

4 Mix the sauce with the pasta and toss. To serve with the sauce on top, add a tablespoonful of olive oil to the pasta, toss, then serve in bowls. Pour on the tomato sauce and top with slices of roast aubergine and flakes of Parmesan.

summer penne

serves 2

1 red pepper

1 gold pepper

125g or 4oz cherry tomatoes

250g or 9oz penne

125g or 4oz asparagus tips

1 tablespoon olive oil

1 garlic clove, crushed

2–3 sprigs of basil, torn

salt and freshly ground black pepper

fresh Parmesan, flaked

1 Halve and deseed the peppers. Place them cut-side down on a grill pan along with the cherry tomatoes. Grill for about ten minutes, or until the peppers are tender and blackened in places. Cool, then cut the peppers into chunky pieces.

2 Start cooking the pasta, following the instructions on the packet. About three to four minutes before the pasta is done, add the asparagus so it will be just tender when the pasta is ready.

3 Drain the pasta and asparagus and put it back in the pan; add the oil, garlic and salt and pepper to taste, and mix gently but thoroughly, then stir in the peppers and tomatoes. Serve topped with basil leaves, and Parmesan, if desired.

All food starting with a 'p' is comfort food:
pasta, potato chips, pretzels, peanut butter,
pastrami, pizza, pastry.

Sara Paretsky

farfalle with onion, spinach & ricotta

serves 2

3–4 tablespoons olive oil

1 onion, finely chopped

1 garlic clove, crushed

100g or 3½oz baby leaf spinach

salt and freshly ground black pepper

grated nutmeg

250g or 9oz farfalle

125g or 4oz ricotta cheese

fresh Parmesan cheese, grated

1 In a covered saucepan, cook the onion in one tablespoonful of olive oil for seven minutes, until tender but not brown, stirring occasionally. Add the garlic and spinach; cook for a minute or two longer, until the spinach has wilted. Season with salt, pepper and nutmeg. Set aside.

2 Meanwhile, bring a large saucepan of water to the boil, put in the pasta and boil until it's *al dente*, following packet directions. Drain and return to the pasta pan.

3 Stir in the ricotta and the spinach mixture. Toss gently, check seasoning, then serve into bowls and top with grated Parmesan.

Bring the same consideration to the preparation of your food as you devote to your appearance. Let your dinner be a poem, like your dress.

Charles Pierre Monselet
Letters to Emily

penne with grilled peppers in sun-dried tomato vinaigrette

serves 4

2 red peppers, quartered

2 yellow peppers, quartered

400g or 14oz penne

salt to taste

3 tablespoons olive oil

2 tablespoons sun-dried tomato purée

1 tablespoon white-wine vinegar

1 garlic clove, peeled and crushed

freshly ground black pepper

freshly torn basil leaves, to serve

flakes of Parmesan cheese, to serve

1 Fill a large saucepan with four litres (seven pints) of water and put it on the stove to heat for the pasta.

2 Place the peppers skin-side up on a grill pan. Put under a high heat for ten to fifteen minutes, until the skin has blistered and blackened in places. Cover and leave until cool enough to handle, then remove the skin, stem and seeds. Cut the flesh into strips.

3 When the water in the saucepan boils, add the pasta along with a teaspoon of salt and give it a quick stir. Briefly put the lid on until the water has come back to the boil, then let the pasta bubble away, uncovered, for approximately eight minutes, or until it is tender but still has some bite.

4 Put the oil, sun-dried tomato purée, vinegar, garlic and a seasoning of salt and pepper into a jar and shake until well-combined for the vinaigrette.

5 Drain the pasta, then put it back into the still-warm pan. Add the peppers. Give the vinaigrette a quick shake, then add it to the pasta and stir gently until well-coated. Serve immediately, or cover and leave until the salad cools to room temperature. Scatter with basil and Parmesan before serving.

spinach tian

This Provençal dish which is rather like a crustless quiche, is named after the earthenware dish in which it was traditionally baked. It's simple to make and is delicious with some goats cheese, country bread and a tomato salad.

serves 4

1kg or 2lb 4oz spinach leaves, washed

2 garlic cloves, crushed

6 eggs, beaten

55g or 2oz freshly grated Parmesan cheese

salt and freshly ground black pepper to taste

olive oil, for greasing the dish

2 tablespoons chopped fresh herbs,
    such as fennel, parsley or chives

1 Preheat the oven to 150°C (300°F or gas mark 2).

2 Cook the spinach, with just the water clinging to it, in a large saucepan for a few minutes, until tender, then drain. Chop and add the garlic, eggs, most of the cheese, and salt and pepper to taste.

3 Put the mixture into a shallow casserole which you have brushed with olive oil, sprinkle with the rest of the cheese and bake for about one hour, or until firm in the middle.

Tomatoes and oregano make it Italian; wine and tarragon make it French... garlic makes it good.
Alice May Brock

mediterranean bake
with pasta shells

serves 4

2 tablespoons olive oil

1 onion, peeled and chopped

1 fennel bulb

1 garlic clove, peeled and crushed

1 red pepper, deseeded and chopped

1 yellow pepper, deseeded and chopped

1 x 400g or 14oz can tomatoes

225g or 8oz conchiglie

salt to taste

55g or 2oz black olives, optional

freshly ground black pepper

125g or 4oz Gruyère cheese, grated

1 Fill a large saucepan with four litres (seven pints) of water and put it on the stove to heat for the pasta.

2 Heat one tablespoon of oil in a medium saucepan. Add the onion; cover and cook for five minutes.

3 Pare away any tough, outer layers of the fennel. Slice the fennel and add it, the garlic, peppers and tomatoes to the onions. Cook, uncovered, for fifteen to twenty minutes, or until all vegetables are tender.

4 When the water in the saucepan boils, add the pasta and a teaspoon of salt and give it a quick stir. Briefly put the lid on until the water has come back to the boil, then let the pasta bubble away, uncovered, for about eight minutes, or until it is tender but still has some bite.

5 Set the grill to high. Drain the pasta and put it into a shallow dish that will fit under the grill. Add the remaining tablespoon of olive oil and toss well.

6 Add the olives, if using, to the vegetable mixture, season to taste, then pour this over the pasta. Top with a layer of Gruyère. Place under the grill until the cheese has melted and is golden brown, and the dish is piping hot right through. Serve at once.

parmigiana

900g or 2lb aubergines,
   cut in 6mm or ¼-inch slices

olive oil

2 large onions, finely chopped

2 garlic cloves, chopped

1 x 400g or 14oz can chopped tomatoes

225g or 8oz mozzarella cheese, sliced

25g or 1oz freshly grated Parmesan cheese

salt and freshly ground pepper to taste

1 Preheat the oven to 200°C (400°F or gas mark 6). Brush the aubergine slices with olive oil, then grill, first on one side then the other, until golden brown.

2 Fry the onion in one tablespoon of olive oil until tender but not browned – about ten minutes. Add the garlic and tomatoes and simmer, uncovered, for ten to fifteen minutes, until thick. Season with salt and pepper to taste.

3 Layer the aubergine, mozzarella and tomato mixture into a lightly oiled shallow casserole, ending with a layer of tomato. Sprinkle with the Parmesan cheese.

4 Bake in the preheated oven for about forty minutes, or until golden brown and bubbling.

In a country called Bengodi... there was a mountain made entirely of grated Parmesan cheese, on which lived people who did nothing but make macaroni...

Bocaccio
Decameron

oven-baked ratatouille

Made from vegetables that roast so well, ratatouille is a natural for the oven. Turn it into a meal by serving with garlic bread (see page 45) or some hot, fluffy couscous and cheese to follow.

serves 2–4

1 large onion (red or purple)

1 large courgette (or 2 or 3 small ones)

1 large aubergine

2 red peppers

4 garlic cloves, peeled and roughly chopped

juice of ½ lemon

2 tablespoons olive oil

salt and freshly ground black pepper

4 tomatoes, quartered

several sprigs of fresh basil

1 Preheat the oven to 200°C (400°F or gas mark 6).

2 Peel the onion and quarter. Trim the courgettes and aubergine and cut each into chunky pieces, about the same size as the onion pieces. Halve and deseed the peppers and cut into similar-sized pieces.

3 Put the vegetables and garlic in a roasting tray, sprinkle with the lemon juice, oil, and some salt and pepper, then mix until well-coated. Put into the oven and cook, uncovered, for twenty minutes.

4 Add the tomatoes and cook for a further twenty minutes. Then tear the basil over the top and serve.

There are many miracles in the world to be celebrated, and, for me, garlic is the most deserving.

Leo Buscaglia

Never eat more than you can lift.

Miss Piggy

puddings

A pudding rounds off any meal – or makes a lovely snack in its own right when you're feeling decadent, or are in need of cheering up. So in this section I've gathered together some lovely, easy desserts that are quick to do and make the perfect ending for a Mediterranean feast. There are some wonderful fruity creations – Hot, Buttery Figs, Chocolate Fondue with Strawberries, An Exotic Fruit Salad, to mention just a few – as well as the easiest ice cream in the world, Watermelon and Vodka Sorbet, and Fast and Wonderful Chocolate Brownies, which really do live up to their name.

fast & wonderful chocolate brownies

Just measuring, melting and stirring are all that's required to make these. Get them into the oven before you sit down to eat and they'll be ready for afterwards, all warm and gooey. Serve with cream, ice cream or thick, natural yogurt.

Makes 15

100g or 3½oz walnut pieces,
  or roughly chopped pecans

100g or 3½oz butter, in rough pieces

100g or 3½oz plain chocolate,
  broken into pieces

225g or 8oz light-brown sugar

2 eggs

55g or 2oz self-raising flour

1 Preheat the oven to 180°C (350°F or gas mark 4). Line a 20cm (eight-inch) square tin well with non-stick paper.

2 Put the nuts onto a baking tray and bake for around six to eight minutes, until they're golden and smell wonderful. Set aside.

3 In a saucepan, melt the butter and chocolate over a gentle heat. Remove from the heat and stir in the sugar, eggs and flour. Beat together until smooth, then stir in the nuts.

4 Pour into the tin and bake for about thirty minutes; the brownies will be firm at the edges and still soft in the middle.

5 Cool for a few minutes, then cut into slices. Remove from the tin with a spatula.

Research tells us that fourteen out of any ten individuals like chocolate.

Sandra Boynton
Chocolate: The Consuming Passion

summer fruit fool

serves 4

225g or 8oz strawberries, stalks removed

225g or 8oz raspberries

225g or 8oz blueberries or blackberries

85g–125g or 3–4oz caster sugar

300ml or 10fl oz double cream, or half cream
and half Greek yogurt, or just yogurt

1 Simply put all the fruits into a saucepan with the
sugar and heat gently for about five minutes, until
the juices run. Remove from the heat and set
aside to cool.

2 If you're using some yogurt with (or without) the
cream, stir this in when the fruit is cool. Whisk
the cream until it's light and thick, then fold it
into the cooled fruit mixture. It doesn't have to be
completely smooth; some purple-red drifts of fruit are
part of the charm.

plums & cream

Often, lots of plums in the shops are not always as sweet and ripe as you'd like. Cook them quickly with some sugar, however, and they become juicy and lovely, especially when served with thick cream.

serves 4

750g or 1lb 10oz plums, any colour

125g or 4oz caster sugar

double cream or thick yogurt, to serve

1 Wash the plums, then put them, with the water still clinging to them, into a saucepan and add the sugar.

2 Place the saucepan over a moderate heat and leave to cook gently for about ten minutes, until they're tender and beginning to collapse.

3 Serve hot, warm or cold.

cinnamon yogurt

This is so simple, but always appreciated. It's delicious on its own or with a fruit salad of fresh dates, sliced bananas, rose water, fragrant rose petals and blanched almonds.

serves 4–6

Large carton thick Greek yogurt

4–6 tablespoons soft brown sugar

1 teaspoon ground cinnamon

1 Mix the yogurt gently until really smooth, then put into a shallow glass bowl and smooth the top.

2 Mix the sugar with the cinnamon, then sprinkle evenly and thickly over the top.

3 Refrigerate until needed.

an exotic fruit salad

2 sweet, juicy oranges

1 large (or 2 small), ripe mango

1 large, ripe pawpaw

2 ripe kiwi fruit

225g or 8oz sweet purple grapes

2 passion fruit, wrinkled and heavy

1 Cut the peel and pith thickly off the oranges, slicing round and round and letting any juice drip into a large bowl. Then cut the juicy segments and put into the bowl. Squeeze any remaining juice out of the remains of the orange, then discard.

2 Peel and slice the mango, pawpaw and kiwi fruit and add to the bowl along with the halved grapes.

3 Finally, cut the passion fruit in half, scoop out the speckled contents, and add.

instant raspberry ice cream

If you've got a food processor, this is an almost magical dish that you can make any time. All you need is a packet of frozen raspberries in your freezer, a carton of cream and some sugar. You can also make a fabulous non-dairy version using soya 'cream', which you can get at most health shops and some supermarkets.

serves 4

275g or 9½oz frozen raspberries

85g or 3oz caster sugar

300ml or 10fl oz single cream

1 Put the frozen raspberries, straight out of the freezer, into the food processor.

2 Add the sugar and cream and whizz. In just a few seconds, you'll have a thick ice cream.

3 Scrape down the edges a couple of times and whizz again briefly, if necessary, to get an even mix, then serve immediately.

I doubt whether the world holds for anyone a more soul-stirring surprise than the first adventure with ice cream.

Heywood Campbell Brown

apple tarte tatin

Put this into the oven before dinner, then it's ready for afterwards. You'll need a 20cm (eight-inch) tart tin or special tarte tatin dish.

serves 4

225g or 8oz ready-rolled puff pastry

juice of half a lemon

5 medium Cox apples

40g or 1½oz butter

40g or 1½oz sugar

cream or crème fraîche, to serve

Good apple pies are a considerable part of our domestic happiness.

Jane Austen

1 Preheat the oven to 200°C (400°F or gas mark 6).

2 Roll the pastry on a floured surface to make it a bit thinner, then cut a circle 1cm (half an inch) bigger than the top of the tin.

3 Peel and quarter the apples and sprinkle with the lemon juice. Melt the butter in a pan and add the apples and sugar. Cook over a high heat for about six minutes, until the apples are slightly browned.

4 Put the apples, round side down, into your cake tin and scrape in all the gooey juice from the pan, too.

5 Put the pastry on top, tucking it down into the apples at the sides. Prick the pastry, then bake for twenty minutes.

6 To serve, loosen the edges with a knife, then invert over a plate. The apples will be on top. Leave to settle for a couple of minutes before serving.

super-fast ice cream

If you put this into a shallow dish in the freezer, you can have some ice cream in about an hour, so it's quite feasible for a quick meal. It's over-sweet, over-rich and wonderful comfort food. Everyone adores it. This recipe makes a lot, but it will keep in the freezer.

serves 8–10

600ml or 20fl oz double or whipping cream

400ml or 14fl oz can skimmed
    condensed milk

1 Whisk the cream until soft peaks form. Use an electric whisk for speed and ease, although you can do it by hand.

2 Add the condensed milk to the cream and whisk again until combined.

3 Tip into a suitable container – a rigid plastic box is ideal – and freeze until firm.

barbecued bananas

4 bananas, slightly under-ripe, skins on

150g or 5½oz chocolate, milk or dark,
   as you please

1 With a sharp knife, make a cut in the top of each banana from end to end, cutting deep into the fruit but not going through the skin at the bottom.

2 Next, open out the slit and pop in the squares of chocolate, dividing them among the four bananas. Wrap the bananas in foil.

3 Place the bananas on the grill over medium coals (or into a moderate oven, if you prefer) for about ten minutes, or until the chocolate has melted and the bananas are lightly cooked.

4 To serve, open the foil packages, pull back the banana skin and eat the chocolatey flesh with a teaspoon, with or without vanilla ice cream on top.

baked apricots
with strawberries

*So often, apricots are disappointingly hard. But if
you bake them in the oven and then mix them with
another seasonal fruits – strawberries, for example –
the result is quite delightful.*

serves 4

500g or 1lb 2oz apricots

125g or 4oz caster sugar

juice of 1 orange

500g or 1lb 2oz ripe strawberries

1 Preheat the oven to 180°C (350°F or gas mark 4).

2 Wash, halve and stone the apricots, then put them into a casserole. Sprinkle with the sugar and pour on the orange juice. Cover with a lid or foil and bake for about forty-five minutes, or until the apricots are tender.

3 Wash and hull the strawberries, then halve or slice them, depending on size, and add to the apricots.

4 Serve at once, or leave to cool.

The strawberry grows underneath the nettle,
And wholesome berries thrive and ripen best
Neighboured by fruit of baser quality.
                              William Shakespeare
                                    Henry V

blackberry &
apple compôte

*You can get apple juice concentrate at health
shops. It makes an effective natural sweetener
for fruit compôtes.*

serves 4

4 eating apples, peeled and sliced

500g or 1lb 2oz blackberries

4 tablespoons apple juice concentrate

honey or sugar to taste, optional

1 tablespoon arrowroot

1 Put the apples into a saucepan with the blackberries and apple juice concentrate and cook gently, with a lid on the pan, for fifteen to twenty minutes, or until the apples are tender.

2 Taste and adjust sweetening with a little honey or sugar as necessary.

3 Dissolve the arrowroot in a tablespoonful or two of cold water, pour into the pan and stir in gently. The juice will thicken almost immediately.

4 Serve warm or cold, with thick yogurt or cream.

Comfort me with apples: for I am sick of love.
The Song of Solomon

hot, buttery figs

serves 4
8–12 ripe fresh figs

55g or 2oz unsalted butter

55g or 2oz soft brown sugar

double cream or Greek yogurt, to serve

1 Allow two to three figs per person, depending on the size of the figs. Cut the figs down from the stem to make a cross shape and open them out, but don't cut so far that they fall apart.

2 Melt the butter in a large saucepan and add the sugar. When it has melted, put in the figs and stir them gently in the buttery mixture over a moderate heat for a few minutes, until they are well-coated and glistening and tender.

3 Serve with lots of cream or thick Greek yogurt.

chocolate fondue with strawberries

55g or 2oz chocolate, plain or milk

2–4 tablespoons cream, single or double

125–225g or 4–8oz strawberries, washed but
   still with their green bits

1 Break the chocolate into a china or glass bowl or
serving dish and melt in the microwave, or set the
bowl over a pan of boiling water until the chocolate
has melted.

2 Remove from the heat and gently stir in the cream
to make the mixture as soft as you want.

3 Put the strawberries into another bowl and serve
with the fondue.

piedmont peaches

serves 4

4 large peaches, halved and stoned

85g or 3oz macaroons, crushed

55g or 2oz caster sugar

40g or 1½oz unsalted butter, plus a little extra
   for greasing the dish

½ teaspoon grated lemon rind

a little water, amaretto or peach brandy

double cream or Greek yogurt, to serve

*An apple is an excellent thing – until you have
tried a peach.*

George du Maurier

1 Preheat the oven to 180°C (350°F or gas mark 4). Butter a shallow casserole which will hold all the peach halves in a single layer.

2 Hollow out the peaches a little more around the cavities where the stone was. Chop the scooped-out flesh and put into a bowl with the macaroon crumbs, sugar, 25g (1oz) of the butter and lemon rind.

3 Mix well so that everything combines, adding enough water, amaretto or peach brandy to moisten the mixture – but don't make it sloppy; use only a teaspoon or two of the liquid.

4 Spoon the mixture into the peach halves, dividing it among them and heaping it up on the peaches. Top with little pieces of the remaining butter.

5 Bake for about thirty minutes, or until very tender. Serve hot, warm or cold, with cream or yogurt.

watermelon sorbet with vodka

The joy of this sorbet is that it never gets rock-solid because of the vodka; in fact, if you add more than the amount given, it won't freeze properly.

serves 4–6

900g or 2lb watermelon cubes

175g or 6oz caster sugar

juice of 1 lemon

1 tablespoon vodka

fresh mint leaves, to decorate

a little extra vodka to serve, optional

1 To get 900g (2lb) watermelon cubes, you'll need half an average-sized watermelon, weighing about 3kg (6½lb). Prepare it by removing all the skin and pips, then dice.

2 Put the melon chunks, sugar, lemon juice and one tablespoonful of the vodka into a food processor and whizz to a smooth purée.

3 Freeze the mixture in an ice-cream maker following the manufacturer's instructions. Alternatively, pour it into a suitable container and freeze until solid around the edges, then whisk or process thoroughly and freeze again until firm.

4 Serve in scoops decorated with mint leaves, and a little more vodka poured over the top if you like.

When one has tasted watermelon, he knows what angels eat.

Mark Twain

Index